ELSTREE AND BOREHAM WOOD PAST

Robert Bard

HISTORICAL PUBLICATIONS

First published 2006
by Historical Publications Ltd
32 Ellington Street, London N7 8PL
(Tel: 020 7607 1628)

ISBN 1-905286-11-2
British Library Cataloguing-in-Publication Data
A catalogue record for this book is available from the British Library
Typeset in Book Antiqua by Historical Publications Ltd
Reproduction by Gilderson, 31 Pitfield Street N1
Printed by Edelvives, Zaragoza, Spain

Acknowledgments

I would like to thank the following people for their interest and help. Firstly John Richardson of Historical Publications for his guidance and direction; Lord Aldenham for checking and providing suggestions on the section relating to Aldenham House, and for allowing and assisting me with the photographing of a number of his ancestral portraits at his home in Dorset; Bob McIntosh of St Nicholas church for opening the church for me on a number of occasions and providing me with much valuable information relating to its history, all offered with patience and humour; Keith Cheyney, archivist at the Haberdashers' Aske's Boys' School for showing me around Aldenham House and its grounds, as well as providing me with some valuable photographs and documents relating to the early history of the house; Rod Brewster, former editor of the *Borehamwood and Elstree Times* for material relating to the history of the paper and of the local police force; Lesley Davies at the Elstree &Boreham Wood Museum for assisting me and for access to her researched works on the history of local schools and libraries; Roxanne Glick of Kemp Row Farm for allowing me to take photographs of the former Hangman's cottage now tastefully incorporated into the main house; Paul Welsh for providing me with much information on Britain's Hollywood; Bob Redman of the Elstree Film and Television Heritage Group for his enthusiastic support; Maureen Keegan, local studies contact, and the staff at Borehamwood Library for their assistance. Eleanor my wife for her patience, support and understanding.

The Illustrations

The following have kindly given their permission to reproduce illustrations:
Lord Aldenham: *29, 30, 31, 35*
Lord Aldenham and Haberdashers' Aske's Boys' School: *27, 28, 36, 38, 42, 44, 45*
Aldenham School: *97, 98*
Borehamwood Library:*6, 7, 47, 49, 52, 53, 54, 55, 56, 62, 64, 65, 66, 67, 68,70, 71, 72, 73, 74, 76,78, 79, 80, 81, 82, 83, 87, 92, 94, 101, 103, 105, 113, 116, 117, 120, 121, 122, 123, 125, 126, 131, 132, 133, 136, 140, 141, 143, 144, 147, 150, 151, 152*
Elstree & Boreham Wood Museum: *48, 69, 84, 89, 90, 91, 134, 154, 155, 156*
Guildhall Library, Corporation of London: *112*
Historical Publications: *5, 26, 51*
National Portrait Gallery: *60, 88, 110*
Radlett Library: *13, 14, 61*
David Robertson: *107*
St Nicholas church: *3*
Verulamium Museum: *2*
All other illustrations were supplied by the Author, Robert Bard

Introduction

Situated 15 miles from the centre of London, Elstree and Boreham Wood today are thriving centres, within the recently created borough of Hertsmere, which also comprises Bushey, Potters Bar and Radlett. As late as 1871 Elstree contained only 525 inhabitants, and Boreham Wood, described as a 'hamlet of this parish' had a population of approximately 800. The growth when it came was due to Boreham Wood's proximity to the railway station which opened in 1868 and provided easy access to London. The combined population of Elstree and Boreham Wood today is approximately 40,000, and the Borough of Hertsmere nearly 100,000.

At the top of Elstree Hill is a cross roads, from which one can see as far as Watford and St Albans. On the right is the old parish church dedicated to St Nicholas, and founded by the monastery of St Albans in 1188. The church was rebuilt in 1360, and again in 1853. It is both the christening and burial place of a number of famous and infamous bygone personalities. Elstree comprises chiefly of a high street which lies on the old Roman road of Watling Street. From the top of Brockley Hill, believed to be the site of the old Roman settlement of *Sullonicae*, one proceeds along Watling Street and up a hill which leads to the village of Elstree. Being situated on the road to St Albans, (Roman *Verulamium*), has meant that Elstree can boast a continuous 2000-year history.

Boreham Wood, as a hamlet of Elstree, has a history going back at least to the Domesday Book of 1086. Theobald Street, which runs from Boreham Wood to Radlett was the original centre of the town. On the surface, little of historical interest has survived the development and housing avalanche that came after the Second World War. However, many buildings of historical interest remain, including Brickfield Cottages, Boreham Wood's first ever school, and farms along Theobald Street that date well into

antiquity. It is hard to believe today that the area along Watling Street approaching Elstree from Brockley Hill and Stanmore was once described as "almost of an impenetrable character, and so much infested by outlaws and beasts of prey, that the numerous pilgrims who travelled along the Roman road for the purpose of devotion at the shrine of Albanus [are] exposed to very imminent danger."

Elstree High Street still retains much of historic interest, although some demolition took place in the 1950s and 1960s. There are houses of medieval origin, and buildings dating from the 15th, 16th, 17th and 18th centuries. The Holly Bush public house is the oldest, Schopwick Place, a fine imposing mansion from *c*.1720, the Artichoke pub is eighteenth-century, and the Plough, now a Chinese restaurant, dates from around 1830.

The original row of trees planted at the request of the first Lord Aldenham during the latter part of the 19th century still marks the route from Aldenham House, along Allum Lane, to Elstree & Boreham Wood station. The former home over 300 years of the Coghills and the Gibbs, is now Haberdashers' Aske's School for Boys – its original gates are in Butterfly Lane. Elstree Aerodrome, at first a grass landing strip for a country club, has managed to keep alive.

Elstree and Boreham Wood have been assisted in retaining the character that sets them apart from London by the extremely active local Green Belt Preservation Society, and the failure in the 1930s to build the Northern Line extension from Edgware. From the top of Elstree Hill, green fields and unspoiled rural landscape abound. Development has been tightly controlled, but is an ever present threat.

In more recent times, Boreham Wood, became the largest centre of film production outside of Hollywood. It has been involved with film since 1914, and the home since the 1920s of the Elstree

1. *The Dury map of 1766 showing Elstree, Boreham Wood and the surrounding area.*

film studios including the now demolished MGM-British complex and Gate Studios. A large number of well-known films were a product of the studios: *2001: A Space Odyssey, Where Eagles Dare, Goodbye Mister Chips. The Dambusters* and *Star Wars* are just a few. The BBC's Elstree Television Centre is the source of a number of well known programmes which include *EastEnders* and *Holby City*. The *Big Brother* series is also filmed in Boreham Wood. The Elstree film industry, actually situated in Boreham Wood, is still very important, a fact which probably does not receive enough recognition.

In writing this history I make no apology for straying outside the tortuous parish boundaries. These seem at times to be illogical. The village itself sat for centuries within four different administrations! Much that we regard as Elstree lies in the parish of Aldenham: Haberdashers' Aske's School, Elstree Aerodrome, and Elstree

(Aldenham) Reservoir are a few examples. The text will include elements of the villages of Aldenham and Radlett simply because they are so close, and contain so much that is integral to the story.

It is my hope to assist the reader in looking at the everyday landscape, streets, and structures of today's Elstree and Boreham Wood, and to look and understand how and why they were formed and obtain an insight into some of the colourful characters that were once a part of this area.

Finally, there is a local sensitivity about how to state the words 'Boreham Wood.' Official signs, the local press, and the Council use 'Borehamwood', but local people tend to use 'Boreham Wood'. Where I am quoting, I have used the spelling as in the quote: otherwise I have used the latter form of the name as a default.

Early Times

The very early period has yielded a few items to suggest human habitation in the area. One possible implement of the Paleolithic period (approximately 500,000 years ago) is a flint flake found in the garden of 60 Lodge Avenue.[1] In Hertfordshire most of the evidence for the Early Mesolithic Period (10,000-6500 BC) is found in the lower Lea and Colne river corridors. At that time the rivers and sea levels were much lower than today and as a result many of the sites are now buried beneath the deep deposits formed as the sea level rose from about 8000 BC. Although these sites are difficult to locate they tend to be well preserved and organic remains such as wood, bone and plants are sometimes found preserved in the deposits. The area around Broxbourne has produced some of the most important early Mesolithic remains in Britain.

Unfortunately, many of the archaeological deposits in the Lea and Colne valleys have been destroyed by development, particularly gravel extraction. The remaining archaeological deposits of this area can therefore be regarded as one of the most critical archaeological assets of Hertfordshire.

Stephen Castle, a respected local historian of the Elstree and Boreham Wood area familiar with its archaeology, sums up evidence of Mesolithic to Neolithic activity: "… a fine example of a flint tranchet axe of this [Mesolithic] period was found in 1984 during the removal of the stump of an oak tree in the back garden of 7, Delamere Road, Boreham Wood, which is on London Clay. The axe, which is datable to *c.* 8500-4000 BC, is now on display in Verulamium Museum, St Albans."

A small assemblage of worked flints was found in the back garden of 53, Lullington Garth, Boreham Wood, between 1980-1988: two flint bladelets, two flint waste flakes and a flint core of Mesolithic or Neolithic (New Stone Age) date and a flint end scraper of Neolithic or Bronze Age date. The garden is on Claygate Beds on the north slope of Woodcock Hill,[2] which is situated on Barnet Lane, an ancient boundary and trackway.

THE LATER MESOLITHIC PERIOD (6500-4500 BC)

During this period water levels rose and Britain finally became cut off from the Continent. In Hertfordshire, inhabitants moved up to the drier land in the upper reaches of the Lea and Colne river system and also began to colonise some of the more heavily wooded areas of the county. We know that Mesolithic man was present in the Radlett area evidenced by a boat found at Old Parkbury, Radlett, in the vicinity of the Colne which was dated by radiocarbon to 5005 BC. Within the boat were the remains of a small child which had been buried in a small box.[3]

2. Mesolithic axe from the back garden of 7 Delamere Road, Boreham Wood, found in 1984.

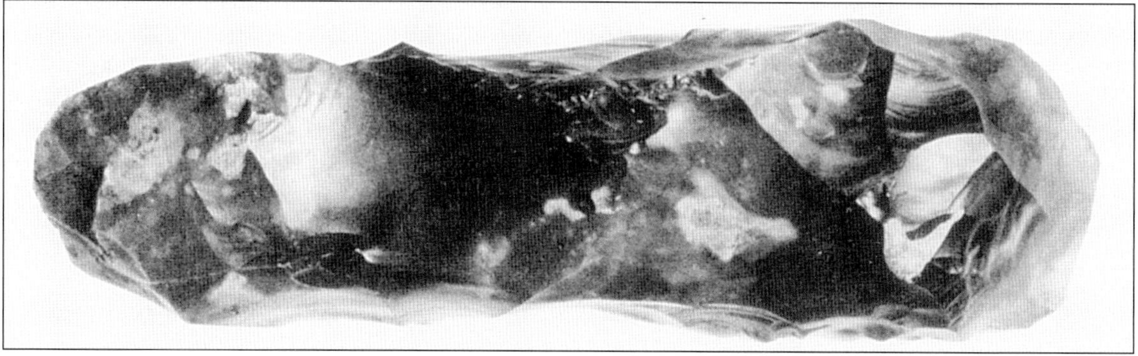

THE FIRST FARMERS

At the beginning of the Neolithic period (4500-2500 BC) methods of crop cultivation and animal husbandry were adopted, allowing people to live in more permanent settled communities. However, this was a gradual process and during the earlier part of the period, farmers were probably still semi-nomadic, mixing hunting with the cultivation of small plots of land and small-scale animal husbandry.

The most impressive surviving Neolithic monuments are the sites which were used for ritual activities and burial. These include the 'long barrows' which are large communal burial mounds, and the large sites enclosed with banks and ditches such as the 'causewayed enclosures' and 'henges' in which ritual and ceremonial activities were carried out.

THE IRON AGE (700 BC - AD43)

By the late Iron Age "Hertfordshire was dramatically transformed from a relative backwater into one of the most important and highly developed areas in Britain ... Further, indeed Hertfordshire is one of the best areas in which to study the late Iron Age in Europe and many of the remains are of international importance."[4] Despite this, and the establishment in AD 10 of the Catuvellauni at nearby *Verulamium* (St. Albans), finds in the Elstree-Boreham Wood area are minimal. Castle comments that evidence is very limited, with only a single piece of pottery having been unearthed. This came from Romeland, a small housing estate in Elstree village situated almost opposite St. Nicholas church. The sherd dates from the late 1st century BC, but could be as late as 1st century AD.

THE ROMANS

Elstree, Radlett and Letchmore Heath have unsurprisingly yielded enough finds to indicate that the area was at the very least an area of much pottery production. The Roman Emperor Claudius I invaded Britain in AD 43, following which Watling Street, running from Dover to Chester, was constructed. Elstree and Radlett are situated on Watling Street in the vicinity of the Roman town of *Verulamium*, and have produced a number of finds, many of which are in the Verulamium Museum. Stephen Castle comments that no physical remains of the road have yet been located in Elstree: "excavations in 1985-1986 immediately to the north of the 15th century Holly Bush, on the west side of the High Street in Elstree Village, found no evidence of the road or its west ditch."[5] It is believed that traces of the original road are still visible, in the form of an agger, or raised bank, in three places: the eastern side of the road at Brockley Hill South, the fir copse at the junction of Elstree Hill North and Allum Lane, and opposite the old Medburn School, just to the north of the the junction of Watling Street and Butterfly Lane.'[6]

Of the nature of Watling Street, its environs, and the true location of *Sulloniacae*, another Roman settlement, which is presumed to lie at the top of Brockley Hill, there was, and has been much debate. It was at one time suggested that *Sulloniacae* may have been in Elstree Village itself. We tend to take the names of Romano-British towns and settlements for granted, but the reality is much different. Very little contemporary Roman information survives that allows us to recognise the present location of towns mentioned in early documents. The key surviving 'roadmap' for Roman Britain is known as the Antonine Itinerary and dates from the 3rd century AD. Its units of 'Roman miles' have led to some confusion and miscalculations as to where places lie, and Elstree's immediate proximity to the Brockley Hill site, a mile to the south, on Watling Street led the antiquary, William Burton (1658) to suggest that Elstree was *Sulloniacae*. In 1970 excavations took place in the grounds of the Royal Orthopaedic Hospital which is situated on Watling Street to the south of Elstree where evidence of a late 1st century AD pottery industry was unearthed. As well as much pottery, coins up to the 4th century were found.

THE KINK AT ELSTREE

There has been some interest amongst academics why, a normally straight road such as Watling Street should kink at Elstree. We are told:

"At Sulloniacis – Brockley Hill – the road turns from north-west to north-east for one mile (1.6 km) to and through Elstree village. There, from another high point (actually in line with the road but not on it, altitude 146m (490 ft) on the Barnet road) where a sighting beacon could be established, the road resumes another long north-westerly alignment direct to *Verulamium*. This one mile detour in the road was the best way to keep the road on high ground. The one mile section between Brockley Hill and Elstree does not go lower than 110m (370 ft), leaving to the right the lower ground … and to the left the lower ground now occupied by the Aldenham and Hillfield Park reservoirs. Beyond Elstree the new alignment is closely followed for 7.5km (4¾ miles) through Radlett to Park Street, but the present road has been much widened and no traces of the old road remain."[7]

Canon Eales, rector of Elstree who wrote a short *History of Elstree* in 1922 makes a number of observations on the Roman connection:

"More than 1950 years ago, the Romans had occupied this country, and were spreading great roads all over it, and building towns and cities from London up to York. Idulfs-tre [Elstree] lay on the direct road between the two. *Sulloniac*, a mile away, lay on Brockley Hill and all around it. Gough, the historian, wrote 300 years ago: 'Coins, rings, urns, and Roman bricks were dug up here when Mr. Napir built his house, and in seven or eight acres round.' This house stood on the left-hand side of the top of the hill, as you go from Elstree to Edgware. Many such remains have been found since, vases and bricks in 1900, some Roman coins in 1915 … The city [*Sulloniac*] was burnt in one of the battles between the Britons and the Romans. Along the road from it to St Albans, Roman houses were built at intervals. The discovery of much Roman pottery at 'Frith Knowl' [in Allum Lane, now demolished] implies that one such house stood there. In Boreham Wood at 'The Firs' more than 100 earthen supports for hot air flues were discovered in 1900. In 1904 a great Roman burial urn was dug up near the road in the field below Mr. Hunt's shop. In the urn was a smaller vessel of Italian work – red clay with a black glaze – also portions of a glass bowl. These point without doubt to the field being a Roman cemetery for the townsfolk of *Sulloniac*. Many similar relics must still be beneath the soil there. The smaller vessels contained food and drink for the spirit of the dead, while the urn held the ashes of the body. …*Penny Well* is in Fortune Lane. It is of Roman origin and perhaps had a statue of the goddess of Fortune over it."[8]

MORE ROMAN FINDS

Between October 1947 and March 1948, Helen O'Neil excavated the remains of a badly disturbed Roman tile kiln in the back garden of Timber Cottage, High Street, Elstree Village. The few sherds of coarse pottery recovered dated from the late 1st or early 2nd centuries. The kiln appears to have produced bonding tiles, *tegulae* (flanged roof tiles), ridge tiles and decorated box flue tiles, the latter used in hypocaust heating systems. Further excavations by the Stanmore, Edgware and Harrow Historical Society in 1948 in 1950 found a number of waste dumps of Roman tiles, sherds of coarse pottery, a perforated

3. Courseware jar with a moulded bead rim, c. 70-120 AD, found in a field to the west of nos. 15-17 High Street, Elstree in 1904. The jar is on display in St Nicholas church.

clay spacer and the torso of a human figure in fired red clay.

Other finds include a scatter of Roman tile fragments and a small circular pit found between 1974 and 1976 in a field opposite Hill House, containing tile fragments of the 1st or early 2nd centuries. Between 1980 and 1983, a vast scatter of Roman tiles was unearthed, with a redeposited *mortarium* rim dating from the late 1st or early 2nd centuries. At 15-17 High Street Elstree, a Roman perforated clay spacer, probably 1st or early 2nd century AD, was found.

At Romeland, an extensive dump of Roman tile waste and clay was discovered.[9] These 1st or early 2nd century AD sherds were found in 1985.[9]

W A Brooks in his undated *History of Elstree and Borehamwood* refers to an abundance of pottery being found near Home Farm in the grounds of Aldenham House, now Haberdashers' Aske's School for Boys. He cites these finds as being a possible link with a 'suspected' local Roman road that "may have left the west side of Watling Street to the south of the crossroads in Elstree village and ran north-eastwards to join up eventually with the pre-historic Icknield Way, near Whipsnade. What could be vestiges of its agger can be traced to the south of Home Farm.[10]

THE SAXONS

AD 410 marks the period after which Britain no longer received support from Rome. The Roman army departed, and many elements of Roman civilisation with it.

Hertfordshire is one of the few areas of southern England which has not produced any significant evidence of early Anglo-Saxon settlers during this period. It is not entirely clear why this is so, although it may be that Roman life continued on in Hertfordshire in some form until the 6th or 7th centuries. This was possibly in the form of a 'British' kingdom centred on the old Roman city of *Verulamium*, but again, there is also little archaeological evidence for this.

Canon Eales attributes the development of Elstree to a Saxon, Edulf and his successors who,

"cleared more forest-land, and used the Roman remains as building material ...Another relic of these times is the Grims Dyke, the great mound and ditch which runs from Harrow to Barnet – a great wall of defence between the lands of different tribes. It is clearest at Harrow, plain on Brockley Hill, easily traced on the Whitchurch side of Elstree Hill South, and to be found at intervals in Barnet Lane as we go towards Barnet. Probably its line determined the boundary between Hertfordshire and Middlesex in later days."[11]

However, there are some indications that the area of Elstree, Boreham Wood and the parish of Aldenham was settled in Saxon times. There is a reference to 'Tidulfes treow', an early spelling of the name Elstree, in Offa's Charter of 785, but there is some doubt as to the charter's authenticity. 'Titebersth', now the area adjoining Theobald Street, is mentioned in Domesday Book of 1086. Finally, Aldenham parish church is of Saxon origin. It is just the more tangible signs of everyday settlement that are evading modern archaeologists.

1   Stephen Castle and W Brooks, *The Book of Elstree & Boreham Wood*, p11.
2   *ibid*, p.11
3   www.hertsdirect.org/libsleisure/heritagel/archaeology
4   *ibid*
5   Castle & Brooks, p12
6   Anthony Frewin, *Elstree & Boreham Wood through two thousand years*, p12
7   O and T Roucoux, *The Roman Watling Street from London to High Cross* (1984). A Dunstable Museum Trust publication
8   A R T Eales, *A Lecture on the History of Elstree*, pp 4-5
9   Castle & Brooks, p13
10   W A Brooks, *History of Elstree and Borehamwood*, p2
11   Eales, p5

Early Records

THE PARISH REGISTERS

The parish registers of St Nicholas, Elstree date back to the seventeenth century. The extracts below record some of the more unusual entries:

1660 Mary, daughter of Charles and Margaret Braint who was killed with the fall of a table. Buried Aug. 22nd.

1661 Hannah Alcocke, who was killed by a fall off the topses of George Carpenter's carte about Wedd Hill.

1662 William Clarke was baptised May 9th, and was borne in the fields nigh Medborne.

1676 Richard Leper died gored by a bull Nov 10th, buried Nov 20th.

1689 Joseph Harris, aged 88 yeares and Parish Clerk about 50 yeares, died March 16th, buried March 9th. Born in the reign of Queen Elizabeth I – grown in the time of James I, Clerk in the days of Charles I, Commonwealth – Charles II, James II, William and Mary

1706 Eleanor Harrison, widow of — Harrison dyed (being found burnt cross her own fire almost to ashes) Nov 7th, was buried Nov 9th, that little part of her that remained from ye fire.

1710 Thomas Angel, a poor traveller sent hither with a pass and dyed the day he came, buried March 3rd.

1710 My dear brother, John Hawtayne, who was a Captain of Foot in her majesty Queen Anne service, died at Amsterdam in Holland of the small pox 23rd of Dec, was buried the 26th day of the same month in the English Church in the Calver Street in that city. My brother died there sent upon business for the publick. Registered here by me Wm Hawtayne, Rector of Elstree this 20th day of January.

1713 Mrs Joyce Vaillant, wife of Mr Paul Vaillant, bookseller of S. Clement's Dane, who was my eldest and most dearly beloved sister aged 37, buried Oct 31st. The above together with Mary and Catherine Susanne Hawtayne, children of the Rector are buried in a vault on left hand side of Chancel under Choir stalls.

1719 Elizabeth Waple, buried March 3rd [her headstone found after being lost for 50 years is now in the church floor].

An unlikely entry is the death of Grace Hale *aged near 180*, buried April 22nd, 1731.

The parish registers covering the period 1655 to 1757 are now in the County Record Office at Hertford. They comprise 126 vellum pages bound in calf. There are a number of gaps, which the Rev. Eales, put down to "clerical carelessness". In 1914 he copied the register into a small volume. He tells us in his introduction that the register had been originated by Mr William Fly, who had been put in place of the Rector, Abraham Spencer during the Protectorate (Spencer was reinstated in 1660). On the first page was the inscription

> "This booke was bought for a Register by Maister Fly of Richard Williams, Stationer, of Saint Albans, which said Mr. Fly, beinge Minister of Elsterie, bestowes this Booke on his Parish. It cost Twentye Shillinges. Dated the eight daye of October, in the yeare of our Lord God One Thousand six hundred fiftye and five."

BABY FARMING

It was a common practice up to the later part of the eighteenth century for babies, illegitimate or otherwise, to be farmed out for wet nursing. Parish registers, not just in Elstree, record what generally tended to be short lives, either from illness or lack of care or nutrition. Some were simply murdered. Eales notes in his 1922 history that,

> "an evil trade was carried on in the parish in the seventeenth and eighteenth centuries – that of baby-farming. The register records many instances of it ... In 1658... 'A child that Goody Rood nursed was buried in ye chancel Sept.11th: another child that Goody Rood nursed – Sept. 22nd.' In 1661 four nurse-children buried and for several years following three or four a year; in 1690 there were six; in 1692 and 1693 ten each year, and each year onwards to 1710 from six to ten. These were mostly local children, but from

that time onwards they began to come from London to be nursed, and to be buried: 1703 (nine); 1716 (sixteen). In 1723 out of twenty-six burials there were twenty-three nurse-children buried and this went on in like proportion for another twenty years or so…..It is a dark stain on the authorities and the parishioners of that time.'[1]

SOME EARLY WILLS

The following wills relate to Elstree and St. Nicholas.

May 10, 1424 "I, Thomas Newchapman, citizen and brewer of London, leave my body to be buried in the Church of St. Nicholas of Ilestr', [Elstree] next the body of the late Rector of the same Church buried. I leave to the high altar of the same church, so that the Rector for the time being may celebrate and pray for my soul, three shillings and four pence … I leave to the high altar of the Church of St. Margaret, of Eggeswer, [Edgware] for my tythes and oblations forgotten, and for praying for my soul, three shillings and four pence."

Jan. 26, 1504 "I, William Roger of Ilstre, yeoman, desire to be buried at Aldenham. I leave to the two altars in Ilstre, two shillings, namely, to the high altar, twelve pence, and to the altar of the Blessed Mary the Virgin, twelve pence."

April 8, 1537 "I John Assheley, of Ilestre, bequethe and recommend my bodie to be buried in the Chapell of our Ladie, within the parisshe church of Seynt Nycholas of Illestre, before the Image of our Ladie within the same chapel.

"I bequethe to the high aulter of the saide parisshe of Seynt Nycholas, for my tythes negligently forgotten or witholdyn, xs.

"I will that myn executeurs cause an honest prieste to celebrate and sing or sey masses, and other prayers and orisons within the parisshe churche of Saint Nicholas, for the welthe of my soule, my good friends' soules, and all Christen soules, by the space of thre hole yeres… and the same preeste to have yerely for his stypende or wages vili. Iiis. Iiid.

"I will that ymediatly after my decease myn executours shall yerely during the lyfe naturall of Jone, my wife, kepe an obyte for the welthe of my soule, my good frendes' soules, and all Christen soules within the parisshe church of Ilestre, expending thereupon to the priestes, clerkes, poor people, and a repast for my executours and their frendes xiiis.iiid. And after the decease of me John, and Joane my wife, I will that a like yerely obyte be holden for me, my sayd wife, and all our good friends, at the said place during the space of xx. Yeres, if the lawes of the realme wyll it so long suffer, expending thereupon xiiis. Iiid. And if the lawes wyll not suffer it, then the said xiiis.iiid. to be bestowed among pore people of the seyde parisshe of Ilestre and other dedes of pite and charite."

Feb. 1591 "Simon Cogdall, of Ilstree, desires to be buried in the Church of Illstree – beqeathes to John Messinger, of Borham Wood, £20 – the residue of property, 'together with my two lesses, one in Tibhurst Street called Tylers, and the other in Borham Wood called Bulhead, to Marryan my wife.' "

Feb. 1600 "Humphrey Roods, of Eilstrey, desires to be buried in the churchyard of Eilstrey. To the poor of the towne, 5s."

1   Eales p17

The Manors

Elstree is not mentioned in the Domesday Survey of 1086. This is subject to some speculation but Chauncy writes that "at the time of the Conquest, [Elstree] was a waste Piece of Ground overgrown with Wood, which is the Reason no mention is made of it in *Domesdei Book*…"[1] Cussans believes that the lack of an entry in the Survey means that "… we may infer that at the time that record was compiled, this parish was waste land, from which the King derived no profit."[2] This seems the most likely reason.

ALDENHAM

This manor was granted by Offa, King of Mercia in 785 to St Peter's Church, Westminster (later to be Westminster Abbey). The land granted was that of Aldenham extending "to the Elstree Woods at that time."[3] St Peter's was granted "the usage, meadows, grazing, fishing, woods that belong to it, including the thick forest land and all related uses that they have …"[4] It seems that around the time of the Norman Conquest in 1066, not all was harmonious in the matter of the manor of Aldenham, for both the abbeys of St Albans and of Westminster laid claim to it. The acrimony of this dispute echoes through the period AD 785 to 1450 when it was decided in a most Christian manner that "the Abbot of Westminster should have the imprisonment of all men arrested in Aldenham, except the men of the liberty of St Albans, and that the gallows erected at Keneprowe [Kemprow] should be common to both abbots for hanging of those condemned."[5]

The conflict was highlighted by Chauncy writing in 1700. He states that around the time of the Conquest, Frederick, the abbot of St Albans, demised the manor to Westminster for the term of twenty years for one hundred shillings and

4. *The Charter of King Offa AD 785, granted land in Aldenham to Westminster Abbey. Tidulfes treow (Elstree) is mentioned. The charter is in the Westminster Abbey library in the form of 10th, 11th and 12th century copies.*

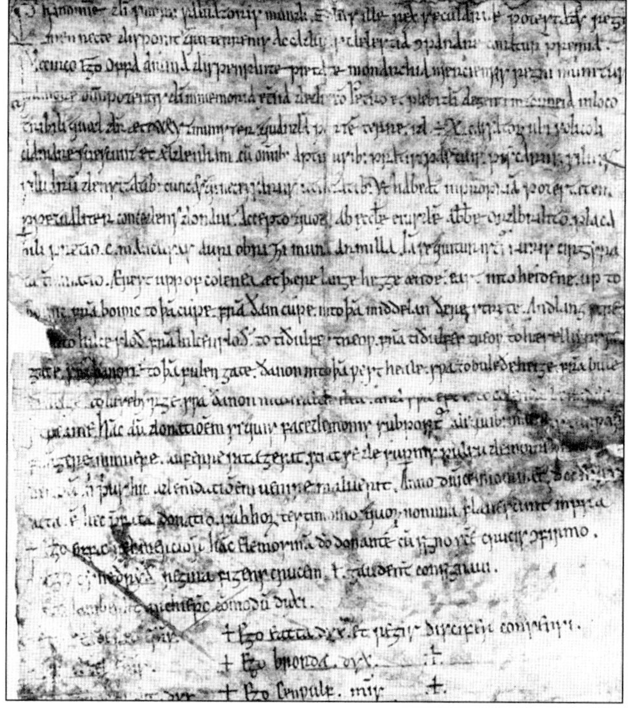

four fat oxen, and that Westminster should keep the lanes and roads safe. However, complains Chauncy, "the Abbot of Westminster, being great at Court, and a Favourite to William the Conqueror, loading him with Presents at his Coronation, he was so elevated that he would not perform his Agreement...." Westminster insisted that some woodland nearby should be part of the agreement, which St Albans refused, and when the term of the agreement expired Westminster declined to give up the manor, claiming that "Abbot Frederick had wrong'd him by detaining the Wood from him, which never belonged to that Mannor; and by crafty Insinuations, and continual Clamours, wherein he was supported by the King's Favour, notwithstanding all that Frederick could possibly do, did hold it in his Possession for divers Years; upon which Frederick ceased to contend any longer."[6]

ELSTREE AND BOREHAM

In 1188 Pope Clement granted to the monastery of St Albans the whole land of Elstree manor and also the wood of Boreham for feeding swine. The monastery kept the manor until the Dissolution, after which it was held by Sir Anthony Denny, a courtier, and then remained in lay hands. By the end of the 18th century it was held by the Phillimore family, who were still in possession by the early 20th century, though much of it was by then enfranchised.

THEOBALD STREET AND THE MANOR OF TITBERST & KENDALS

Theobald Street, which runs from Boreham Wood to Radlett, was originally a manor in its own right, mentioned in Domesday six times and then called Titeberst or variations of that spelling. After the Conquest it was in the hands of Westminster Abbey until the Dissolution. "Its origins and its boundaries have not been clearly established, but it is thought to have extended eastwards towards Shenley or even as far as Ridge at one time, and south from Harper Lane as far as Medbun."[7] Cussans in his *History of Hertfordshire* (1881) gives us interesting details concerning Titeberst which leads via a long and tortuous historical route to the once prominent Phillimore family and Kendal Hall, now Radlett Prep School in Watling Street, Radlett.

1   Chauncy p372
2   Cussans, p75
3   *Victoria County History of Hertfordshire* p349
4   David Robertson, *History of the Manor of Aldenham in Hertfordshire* (1993), p5
5   *ibid*, p6
6   Chauncy p365
7   Wratten, *The book of Radlett & Aldenham* (1990), p31

National Happenings

THE BLACK DEATH

The plague swept Europe in 1347 and arrived in the Elstree area in 1349. No figures exist for the number who died here, but in Park, a manor of St Albans Abbey, of which Elstree and Boreham Wood were a parcel, the manor court book records that 85 out of 150 tenants, including 22 women, had died. Elstree itself, from its higher altitude, might have escaped more lightly.

THE REFORMATION

Land ownership throughout the country was changed enormously at the Reformation instigated in 1534 by King Henry VIII. Church lands were gobbled up by the Crown and then sold on to lay people or organizations. Locally, St Albans abbey was the ruling landlord, and in the case of the Elstree area much of it was taken by the Crown and then *c.* 1542 was sold on to Anthony Denny, one of the Gentlemen of the King's Privy Chamber, and Joan Denny his wife.

CIVIL WARS

The Civil Wars, pitting King against Parliament, lasted from 1642 to 1651. The events left ripples in our local history.

The evidence suggests that Elstree was Parliamentarian, but despite this two ancient monuments were defaced by Cromwell's soldiers *(see illustration of Crowmer monument on p26)*. Sanderson, in his *History of Elstree School*, says that there was a skirmish in the village between the opposing forces. One of the Roundheads left his sword and jacket in a school cellar where they were found in the late 1890s and given to one of the boys. Canon Eales notes that "in the later Civil War there was an engagement when forces from St Albans met some royal troops between Elstree and Edgware, and the latter were driven back with some loss."

5. *Oliver Cromwell, from the painting by Robert Walker, c. 1649, who stayed at Brockley Hill House.*

Kingston's *Hertfordshire during the Great Civil War* relates:

"In the opening days of June 1646 there is much confusion in the county on all sides. Col. Alban Cox and Major Barber are beating up forces for Parliament, but cannot be in all places at once. So the people themselves have to stand on their guard whenever the Royalist troops make their appearance. The first notable skirmish of this kind happened at Elstree, where the Edgeware and Elstree men rose in sufficient numbers to overpower the royalists and took some of them prisoner. The soldiers were sent as prisoners to Hertford Gaol, and the Edgeware and Elstree men for their prowess were awarded the arms taken from the Royalists and some of the horses, the best of the latter being ordered to be sent up to London for the service of the State."

At the parish church Abraham Spencer was ejected from his living and although offered the post again after the Restoration he had by then lost his senses and as Clutterbuck (1815) notes, was 'incapable of subscribing under the Bartholomew act in the year 1662'.

Canon Eales asserts that Oliver Cromwell occasionally used Brockley Hill House as a country residence during his protectorate.

The Parish Churches

ST NICHOLAS, ELSTREE

Sir Henry Chauncy in 1700 wrote that "This Church is situated near the Street, upon a great Hill in a small Churchyard, in the Deanery of St. Alban, in the Diocese of London, and has one Isle, divided from the Body with a Wooden Building at the West End thereof, in which hang three small Bells." A local directory, 1832, describes the church as 'a mean building without anything in its interior worthy of notice.'

But the church was entirely rebuilt in 1853 and a directory of 1854 was able to be more fulsome in its description:

> "The church, dedicated to St. Nicholas, was entirely rebuilt in 1853, with the exception of four pillars, and completely repaired, at a cost of about £3000, entirely supplied by the rector and his friends. A new organ was also added. It is in the early English or decorated style, with a chancel altogether new, extending a few feet beyond the site of the old church. The present structure is of flint, with stone facings. There are 200 free seats. A stained glass window was put in by the children of the National School: a remarkable instance of good feeling towards the church. However, a rather awkward circumstance occurred here respecting its being rebuilt. On the 6th of February, 1854, a couple came to be married, but the chancel being new, and not consecrated, the ceremony could not take place. To avoid the expenses of another consecration, the four old pillars had been left; this might have carried the point, but the chancel being new, and beyond the original limits, the Bishop of London had scruples as to the legality of the marriage. The rector kindly proceeded to Edgware, where he married them."[1]

An 'Old Inhabitant' who published *A Guide to Hertfordshire* in 1880, notes that on the south wall was a handsome monument to Samuel Nicoll Esq, who died in 1723, aged 42; and on the north wall was one to Emily, wife of the Rev. G. Phillimore. At the east end was a stained glass window in memory of the Rev. J. Morris, the late

6. St Nicholas, parish church of Elstree at the end of the 18th century. This illustration is from the period when the church was described as a 'mean' structure. The building underwent substantial alterations in 1824.

7. The remodelled St Nicholas church in 1849. It was taken down in 1853.

8. St Nicholas church interior, 2006.

Rector who died in 1848, erected by his pupils. The walls were stenciled, and scripture texts were inscribed over the arches, of which there were four on each side.[2]

MYSTERY OF THE MISSING CHURCH

Early records suggest that there may have been a second church or chapel in Elstree. The existing church is the third on the same site, but there is a reference in a letter dated 1188 from Clement III to Abbot Warin referring to the chapel of St. Bartholomew.

Again, there is a reference in a charter of Henry III to the Priory of Smithfield (1253). There is debate as to whether the churches were one and the same or existed side by side.

"There they have 2 crofts lying in the parochial de Boshey, and they pay 2s 6d a year on the feast of St Bartholomew at the chapel of Idelstre". This is from a document dated 1306.'[3] Stephen Castle says of this entry that it "is the latest known reference to the Chapel of St Bartholomew at Elstree and, while it is clear that it was on the Middlesex side of the county boundary, its precise location remains a mystery. Excavations in 1974-1976 and 1980-1983 in the large field opposite Hill House, at the west side of Elstree Hill South, failed to locate the Chapel but provided evidence of occupation in the 13th and 14th centuries."[4]

The Rev. Eales, writing in 1914, tells us that "The late Lord Aldenham found foundations near the Reservoir, which he thought belonged to some such building. There has been speculation that a second church, if it existed, was situated in the fields opposite Hill House. There was also a Chantry at Deacon's Hill, granted by Henry VIII to All Souls, Oxford, and a House in Elstree High Street in 1637 called Chappel House."[5]

INTERIOR FEATURES

Eales in his 1922 *History of Elstree* notes that the following are worth looking at:

The pillars, especially on south side; there are masons' marks on them.
The old roof timbers.
The font (1460): the iron cramps by which it is used to be locked up on the top rim: the hole for candlestick at baptisms.
The south doorway (1460), arms of St. Albans Abbey, and rose of King Henry VI.
The coffin plates of Sharpe family by vestry door: two of their monuments in porch.
The monument of Olive Buck (1603) on north wall (I moved this into the church from the porch in 1900): inscriptions in English, Latin, and French.
All the porch monuments were once in the church and ought to be there now.
The stone of Elizabeth Waple (1719). I found it doing duty as a hearthstone in a cottage and placed it by the pulpit.
The black marble stone of Ralph Linch (1730) and his daughter Susanna (1718), dug up in the churchyard and replaced where it belongs by the lectern.
And the marble stones from the Temple of Diana at Ephesus, by organ chamber. These St.Paul must have seen when he preached there (Acts xx)."[6]

The Lych-Gate was given by the Trevor Dawson family at the end of the nineteenth century. Sir Arthur Trevor-Dawson was First Lord of the Admiralty, and the family lived at Edgwarebury, a classic mock Tudor building which is now a hotel and restaurant.

The main doorway into the church pierces the oldest wall of the church, dating from 1188. The wall has against all odds survived the many renovations and rebuildings.

The stone font is of fifteenth-century origin and has been used by a number of well known

9. The section of Matthew Paris' 13th-century Chronica Majora *in which he mentions the* capella *at* Tidulvestre *(Elstree) – see line 2, and the common pasture at* bosci de Borham *(Boreham Wood) – see lines 4 and 5.*

10. *South doorway of St Nicholas, made in 1460. It displays the arms of St Albans Abbey and the rose of Henry VI.*

11. *The St Nicholas font in which Sir Richard Burton, the famous explorer, was baptised.*

people, including Charles Dickens who was the godfather to one of William Macready's children, and the future explorer, Sir Richard Burton, who was baptised here *(see p45)*. The font cover dates from 1974.

The Baptistry window bears the signature of Sir Ninian Comper (1864-1960), a flamboyant Anglo-catholic, art nouveau architect and designer who worked on churches worldwide including Derby Cathedral.

The oldest memorial in the church is to Olive Buck, dated 1603, is extremely fragile and at the moment is encased, and thus not visible.

The Church contains a First World War Memorial which Dr Bill Elliott, rector of St Nicholas between 1974 and 2000 notes is made of a high quality copper plate, but the names on the plate are at some variance to those on the village war memorial! In addition there is a brass to a Capt. Donald T Gorman, M.C which dates the end of the First World War to 1919, and

his cap badge is clipped into the bottom of the shield. The Chancel Screen was given by George Louis Monck Gibbs, brother of Lord Aldenham who lived at Deacon's Hill in Barnet Lane. As Dr Elliot notes, "the screen was originally much higher but was cut down and the spare pieces disposed of in the 1960s. There was a strong fight in the parish to keep it, which went to St Albans Consistory Court, and failed. George Gibbs died as the result of a hunting accident." As well as the screen, George Gibbs donated the organ in 1880.

There is a memorial erected to Sir Harry Hague the proprietor of the Ovaltine Company. Dr Elliot paints a formidable picture of his wife, Lady Hague. As late as the 1950s she always rode side-saddle through the village and if a passing schoolboy did not raise his cap she was into the school to have him brought out on the stage by the Head Master.

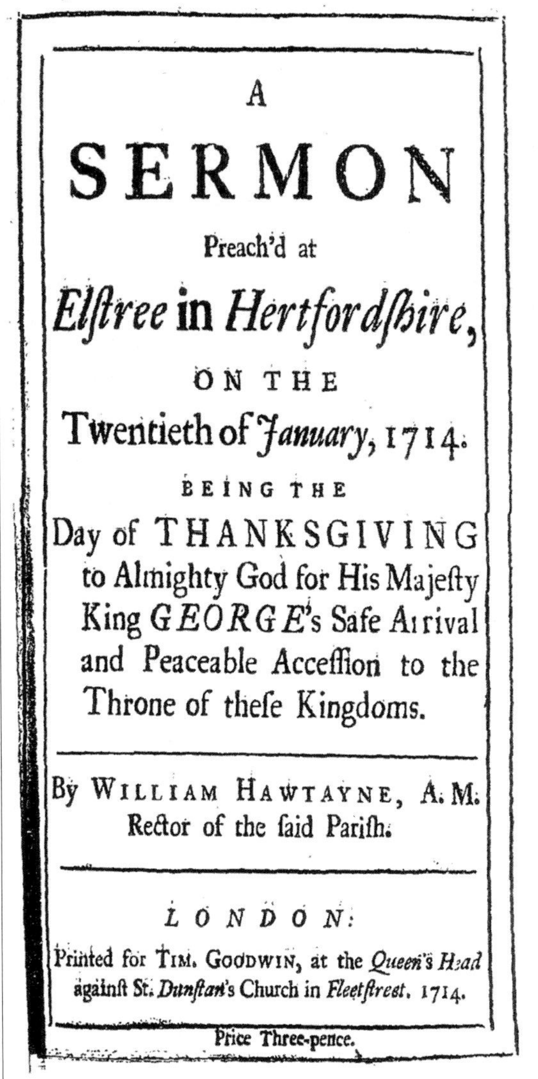

12. *William Hawtayne, rector of Elstree, preached a sermon in 1714 welcoming the 'safe accession' of George I. The king would have been unaware of Hawtayne's sentiments as he never learned to speak English.*

THE VICARS AT ELSTREE

Canon Eales, Rector of Elstree from 1898 to 1945, researched some of the earlier incumbents which he hand wrote into a book in 1914 that also details some of the history of St. Nicholas and reproduces the original parish registers for the period 1655-1757 – these are now in the county record office in Hertford.

Of the clergy he says

"They seem to have been quiet men for the most part, who said their services, visited their flocks, and wrote their records, from which we can gather names and happenings to-day. John Boyle in 1618 became Bishop of Cork. Hugh Jones, under Queen Elizabeth, joined with his parishioners in fitting out soldiers against Spain, the rector contributing a caliver [musket] as his share. Poor Abraham Spencer in Cromwell's time was turned out of church and home for loyalty to Church and King, but he returned in 1660 at the Restoration. William Fly, who was appointed by Parliament, was a Churchman at heart, though he kept it quiet. He bought our parchment register which begins in 1655, and recorded in it that he baptized his child on Easter Tuesday. In those unsettled times marriage was regarded as a civil contract and was legally valid without any religious ceremony, but William Fly remarried all those who had been united by the magistrate, thus giving them the Church's blessing. Samuel Clarke (1740-85) was the only one who seems to have no care at all for his parish. He held a valuable curacy at Hampstead and left the parish to the care of Rev. Mr. Dalton, headmaster of Elstree School. The latter could not take an evening service, "as the parents of his scholars came to see them on Sundays." The churchwardens reported to the archdeacons annually for forty years, "our minister is non-resident, neither have we a curate resident." Again, 'all is well except the minister, and he don't due proper duty, and he as chose a churchwarden that the parish don't a prove of.' But nothing was done until the day of his death."[7]

ST JOHN THE BAPTIST, ALDENHAM

There are a number of reasons for including Aldenham parish church in a history which deals primarily with Elstree, and Boreham Wood. For centuries a part of Elstree fell within the parish of Aldenham, and the Hucks Gibbs family, (Baron Aldenham), which lived within the parish of Aldenham, was inextricably linked with Elstree, which it moulded and changed.

The church is of Saxon origin, though nothing

13. *St John the Baptist, the parish church of Aldenham, c.1812. From an illustration in Kenneth Gibbs' book of parish register entries, dated 1903, kept at Radlett Library.*

14. *Interior of St John the Baptist, 2006.*

15. *Aldenham parish church. The steeple was badly damaged by a bomb during the last war, as were a number of headstones in the churchyard – the latter can still be seen.*

from this period survives within its structure. It is the burial place of many of Elstree's most prominent citizens, including members of the Gibbs and Coghill families. The church also contains a number of very beautiful, exquisitely created memorials as well as some of the finest brasses in Hertfordshire dating from the period 1450 to 1608 and there is a splendid well-preserved monument that deserves a visit. The *Victoria County History* states that

"the earliest evidence for the church is given by a small twelfth-century window in the west wall of the south aisle, which though completely 'restored' appears to be in its original position. If so the church must have had a nave and a south aisle at least, of much the same size as at present, in the twelfth century. Of the early chancel no traces remain. The west tower was added at the beginning of the thirteenth century, and shortly afterwards the chancel was rebuilt and a south chapel added to it. About 1300 the

south chapel was extended eastward, and the chancel was likewise lengthened, to regain the side-light lost by the extension of the chapel.'[8]

A CHURCHLY ABOMINATION

Cussans writing in the 1880s says that because of the way in which additions had been made over centuries, often with little regard to the previous structure, and particularly of a gallery removed during later restorations:

"the building…whether viewed internally from the east or the west, has an awkward one-sided appearance, which immediately strikes a visitor. The beauty of the church is further marred by a most objectionable gallery, containing three large pews, which stretches diagonally from the west wall of the nave, over the west end of the north aisle. It is easy to imagine how, a hundred and fifty years ago, such a repulsive excrescence was allowed to be erected, at the instance of some rich man, who wished to have, and undoubtedly paid for, a private box, in which he, and his family, could

16. *The font at Aldenham church. It is made from Purbeck marble and survives from the 1250 church. There is a domed wooden cover which dates from the Tudor era.*

17. *The parish chest at Aldenham church; "... the finest parish chest I ever saw. It is nine feet eight inches in length and carved out of a solid piece of oak" wrote John Cussans in the 19th century.*

sit, removed from the vulgar crowd; but it is most difficult to conceive, how in this present day such an abomination should be permitted to remain."[9]

Next to the ancient font is a solid oak carved chest bound with a latticework of 5-inch iron bands. The age of this is unknown but the church literature notes that when it was opened its contents included "Vestry Minute Books from 1784, churchwardens' accounts from 1728 and a copy of letters patent granted by Queen Elizabeth I to R. Platt dated the 18th February in the 38th year of her reign for the founding of a Grammar School and Almshouses. It was clearly used as a parish strongbox ...." Cussans comments that

> "In front of the large double monument is the finest parish chest I ever saw. It is nine feet eight inches in length, carved out of a solid piece of oak. It is strengthened with thick bands of iron, crossing each other at frequent intervals. The lid has seventeen massive hinges, and is secured by eight hasps, besides locks, and an iron bolt.."

BRASSES

Brasses in English churches date from 1277, continuing well into the 17th century. Those that remain in the floor of Aldenham church reflect the style of portraiture and clothing from the period of 1450 to 1608. According to the *Victoria County History:*

> "the style of the figures shows that the majority fall within the years 1450-1530. Two in the chancel preserve their inscriptions, those of Lucas Goodyere, *[see ill 19]*, a late sixteenth-century brass with a figure of a woman in a shroud, and Nicholas Chowne, 1569, where the inscriptions and arms ... alone remain. Of the rest the figures of Edward Brisko, 1608, and

18. The earliest brass in Aldenham church, c.1450. There are six daughters portrayed, but only nine feet.

Helen his wife, can be identified from Clutterbuck's description in 1813, when they were on an altar tomb since destroyed, and in the chancel is the indent of an armed figure with two shields bearing the arms of Stepney ... Other figures in the chancel are those of a man and his wife with two sons and six daughters *(ill 18)*; another of a lady, and another group of man and wife with five sons and six daughters...In the vestry is part of the palimpsest brass of John Long, 1538, inscribed on a fifteenth-century plate."[10]

The oldest brass lies in the floor of the Chancel in front of the Sacrarium step. This is a brass to a man, his wife, their two sons and six daughters,

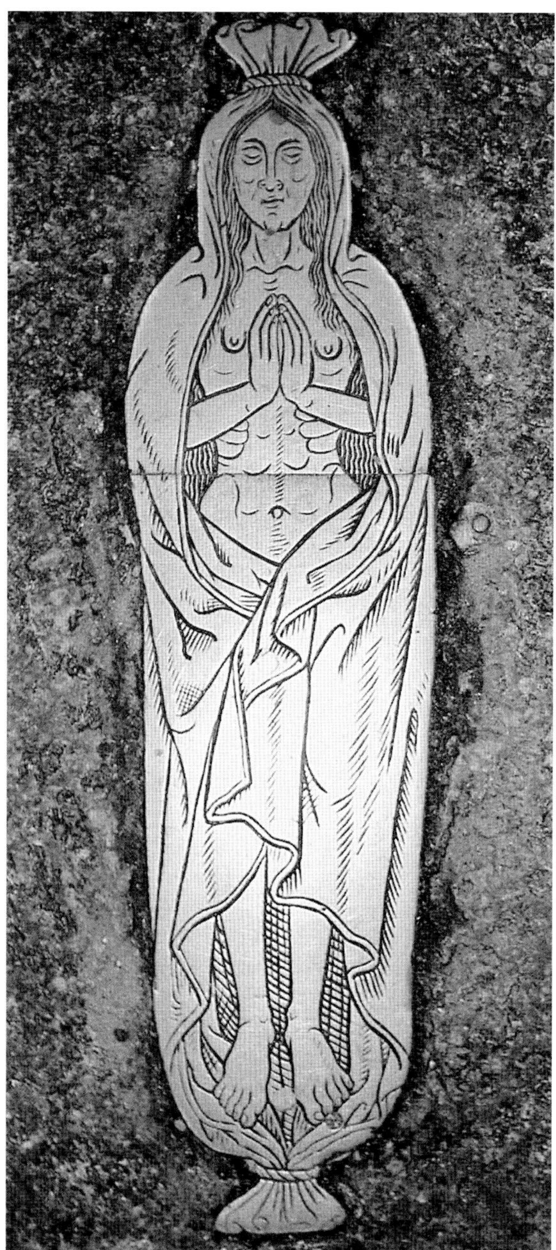

19. *The Goodyere brass in the chancel of Aldenham church. It marks the resting place of Lucas Goodyere and her son Edmond, who both died in 1547. The figure is depicted in a burial shroud.*

and is remarkable for the fact that there would seem to have been an early accounting error: beneath the six daughters should be twelve feet, however there are only nine.

Another brass, that of Lucas Goodyere lying in her shroud is a reminder of the dangers of childbirth in earlier times. Lucas Goodyere died in childbed with her son Edmond, and the inscription underneath the brass itself reads:

HERE UNDER THIS MARBLE STONE LYETHE LUCAS GOODYERE DEP' YD AND GONE, IT PLEASYD THE LORD GOD IN OCTOBRE THE TENTH DAY, SHE BEING IN CHYLDBED DECESYD WITHOUT NAYE, AND EDMOND HIR LITTLE SONNE LYETH HIR BY (on whos sowlys Iesu have mercy. 1547)

The last line and date disappeared sometime between 1700 and 1880.

MEMORIALS

Probably the finest monument is that of John Coghill and his wife Deborah who died within a few weeks of each other in 1714. This memorial took a post-mortem journey across the church. A painting of the church at the beginning of the nineteenth century shows the monument standing in the Lady Chapel, where earlier Coghills are buried. It is now situated underneath the window in a tiny lobby off of the north chancel aisle. John Coghill was the second son of Henry Coghill, a wealthy London merchant and a Sheriff of the County.

20. *The bas-relief memorial to Robert and Sarah Hucks in Aldenham church. It is situated on the south wall*

21. *John Coghill and his wife Deborah, who died within a few weeks of each other in 1714. They lived at Wigbournes, later to become Aldenham House.*

22. *One of the two Crowmer monuments (see next page) in the Lady Chapel of Aldenham church. They date from c.1400.*

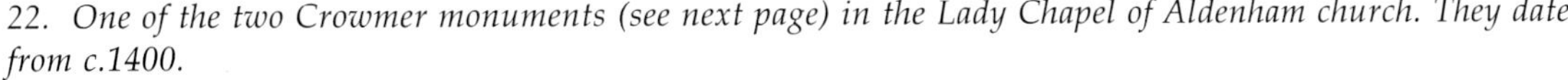

23. *Detail from the Cade memorial in Aldenham church. The Cades were one of the early families to own Penne's Place in the grounds of Aldenham House.*

THE CROWMER MONUMENT

On the south wall of the chancel, under flat-arched canopies, are the recumbent effigies of two females, who are thought to be the wife and daughter-in-law of Sir William Crowmer. They form a single monument. Chauncy in 1700 wrote that "In the South Wall of this Church, the Proportion of two Women lie cut in Stone, who (as I have it by Relation) were two Sisters here intombed, the Founders of this Church, and Coheirs to this Lordship, which at their Deaths gave the said Lordship to this Abby and Convent of Westminster." "The costume of the figures," observes Mr. Cussans, "shows that the monument was erected towards the end of the reign of Edward II ... perhaps as late as the year 1400, but certainly not ten years later. The arrangement of the arms shows that the ladies were not the two wives of one man, nor were they sisters."[11]

However, the church literature says:

"This beautiful monument shews the recumbent effigies of the wife and daughter-in-law of Sir William Crowmer, who was son of John Crowmer of Aldenham. He was Lord Mayor of London in 1413, two years before the battle of Agincourt, and a contemporary of Dick Whittington. Crowmer himself held office a second time in 1423. The costume of the figures shows that the monument was erected towards the end of the reign of King Richard II [1377-99]."

There has been some damage to the tombs at some time. It is possible that some of this was caused by Cromwellian troops during the Civil War. The *Victoria County History* tells us with regards to the heraldry that it was 'unfortunately "restored" in 1840 by a stonemason, and much damaged.'[12]

THE CADE MONUMENT
This is situated in the oldest part of the church, the Lady Chapel. High up in the right hand corner is the figure of Katherine Cade who died in 1615. As with the Coghill monument, her monument was moved during the 19th century

24. All Saints church, 2006.

from her original position on the opposite side of the chapel, facing to the east. The church literature observes that "she was moved to her present place when the priest's door was uncovered and it was found that she blocked the upper half of the doorway. From her inscription we learn that she was 'descended of the ancient family of Throckmorton, a slightly dubious pedigree since the earlier members of the family were all involved in plots and insurrections...'" The Cade family were early proprietors of the Penne's Place estate *(see p31)*.

ALL SAINTS, BOREHAM WOOD
All Saints in Shenley Road was built in 1909 and consecrated in December 1910 to cater for Boreham Wood's rapidly expanding population. It is built on land sold by Elstree parish to developers in 1890, with the plot that the church now stands on being specifically reserved for the purpose. The tower, added in 1957, has a clock on each side. The clocks are replacements for the original ones which malfunctioned so that Boreham Wood had a 72-minute hour.

1   Craven & Co. *Commercial Directory*, 1854, available at Borehamwood Library.
2   *A Guide to Hertfordshire* by An Old Inhabitant, Simson & Co. 1880.
3   Rental of the Priory of St Bartholomew, Easter 1306, at the Bodleian Library
4   Castle & Brooks, *The Book of Elstree & Boreham Wood*, p 23
5   A R T Eales, *The First Register Book of the Parish Church of Elstree*, 1655-1737 (1914).
6   Eales, *A Lecture on the History of Elstree*, 1922, p24.
7   *Ibid*
8   *Victoria County History of Hertfordshire*, p158
9   Cussans, Vol. III, p250
10   *Victoria County History of Hertfordshire*, p160
11   Cussans, Vol. III p251
12   *Victoria County History of Hertfordshire*, p159

26. *William Charles Macready in the role of Virginius. From an engraving by Charles Picart, after a drawing by I. Jackson, RA.*

drowsiness; recovering, considered and wrote down what I thought it proper to say, if requisite to speak, to the audience on the night of my reappearance. Read prayers to the family. I pray Almighty God to forgive my transgressions, and extend His merciful protection to me for the sake of those so justly dear to me.

1839 April 30th. — Went to Elstree in the carriage with Catherine and Willie; enjoyed to a degree I cannot describe the air, the freedom, the sight of the country, and the old familiar objects of my passage to and from Elstree; it was luxury, quiet, ease, content; it was happiness. I could only liken my sensations to those of a person first tasting the fresh and genial air from the long confinement of a sick room, or the captivity in a prison. It was delightful. Surprised to find Elstree, that used to look so pretty, now appear close, flat, shabby! Thus we judge of all things in this world, – ah, how unwisely! — by comparison; the glory in the grass, the splendour in the flower, the delicious breath of heaven, and its gorgeous vision of cloud, and star, and sun, are everywhere the same.

1840 March 4th. — I went with Nina and Letitia to Elstree. My journey was a melancholy one; every familiar object on the road, the road itself, leading over Brockley Hill, as I caught it in the distance, looked as if part of the happy thoughts that were associated with what I think of as my home of many happy years. How often in coming here have I left care, and evil passion, and degrading thoughts behind me, and felt, as the beauty of the landscape opened, and the inspiring freshness of the air breathed on me, my heart spring up and burn within me in gratitude to God and love of His works seen, heard, and felt around me! I must leave it — my home, my home! Farewell, dear, dear Elstree!

1848 September 1st. — Went with Catherine and four eldest children to Elstree: enjoyed the ride with them, the beauty of the country, the recollection of every house and tree, the wandering over and through our old house, Elm Place, where so many of our children were born; walked through the neglected grounds, and marked the shrubs and trees, now grown very high, that I had planted. How many happy hours have I spent there! — and it is consecrated by its sorrows too. I have suffered as well as enjoyed. Walked down to the reservoir: every step was a memory. Went to Mr. Howarth's; dined there.

Aldenham House

Aldenham House still stands almost in its entirety, situated behind the ornamental gates at the bottom of Butterfly Lane, Elstree. It is now the property of Haberdashers' Aske's School, and despite its chequered history, at times neglected, the house retains much of the essence of its 18th and 19th-century character and is now well looked after. The school employs an archivist who conscientiously preserves and researches both the past of the house, and the ex-pupils of the school, which transferred from Hampstead, north London to Elstree in 1961 *(see p75)*.

THE PENNE FAMILY

The estate has a history back to the thirteenth century and Reginald de la Penne. He is recorded in 1275 as holding two acres of land and paying 12d a quarter rent. The Penne family appears frequently in the Aldenham court rolls. Not all of the records are complimentary – in 1394 Richard atte Penne was fined 2d, for being a "fraudulent supplier of ale". The Penne family disappear from the records in 1485 and the estate then passed to the Coningsby family until 1640.

Penne's Place was situated in the grounds of what is now the Haberdashers' school. The presumed whereabouts are recorded on Ordnance Survey maps as being close to the junction of Butterfly Lane and Aldenham Road in the vicinity of what is now a rugby field. There are still traces of the moat visible just inside the main, north Haberdasher gates in Butterfly Lane.

THE COGHILLS

The house we see now was begun by Henry Coghill in the 1630s on the site of a Tudor mansion

27. The location of Aldenham House, as shown in a plan belonging to Robert Hucks, and dated 1794.

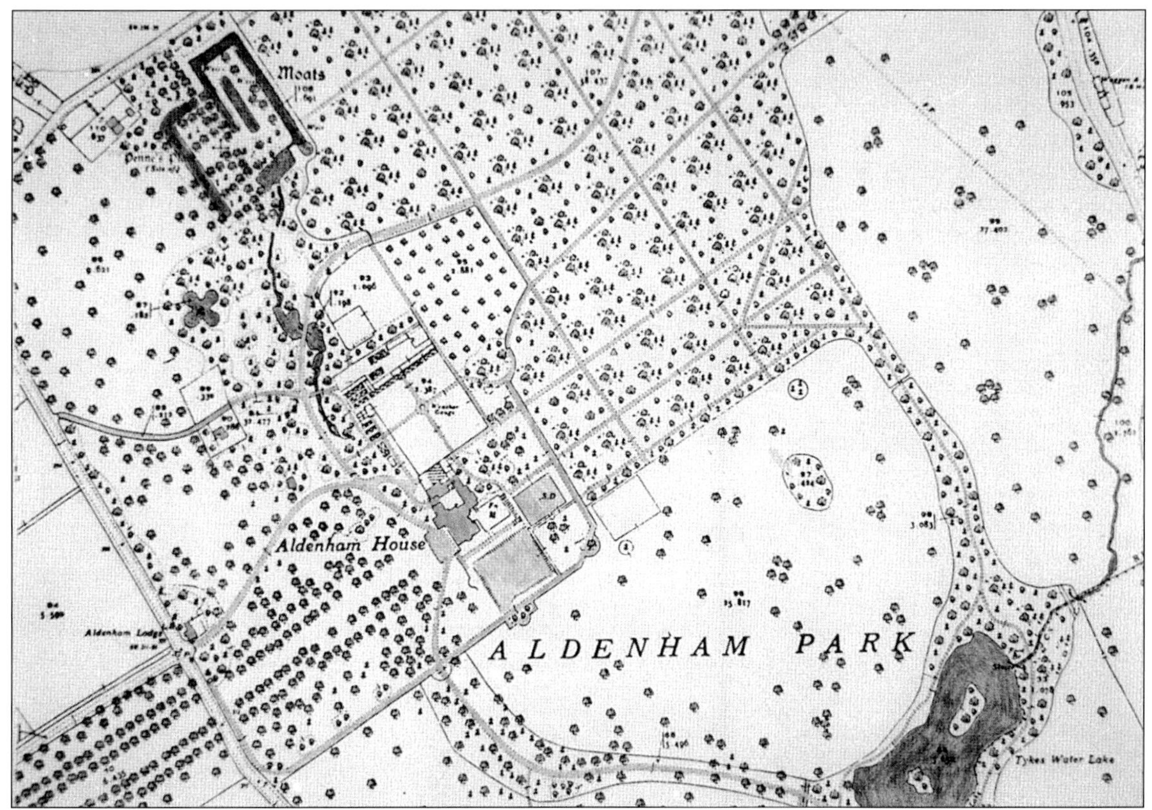

28. Aldenham House in 1786. The drawing was requested by Robert Hucks.

29. Faith Sutton, daughter of a wealthy London merchant taylor, married Henry Coghill who built the original Aldenham House in the 1630s.

called Wigbournes, a name that was continued in use. Coghill had married a wealthy London merchant taylor's daughter, Faith Sutton, and thereby acquired the estate. He then purchased the neighbouring mansion of Penne's Place.

Coghill's allegiance during the Civil War is unknown, but the fact that he retained his estate through these troubled times suggests he was at the least, diplomatic. Henry Coghill died in 1672, two years after his wife.[1] The house remained in the Coghill family until 1728 when it went on the death of the last Henry Coghill to his uncle Thomas who died without an heir. The estate then reverted to Henry Coghill's sister Sarah, who was married to a Robert Hucks of Great Russell Street.

THE HUCKS GIBBS

Sarah Hucks had already inherited Penne's Pace from her brother, and six years later, she received Wigbournes as well and changed its name to Aldenham. She also installed the Venetian window to the left of the west front. Robert Hucks, a Member of Parliament for Abingdon, died after a long illness at the age of 45.

The parish register records Sarah's kindness in befriending Mary Ratcliffe, the daughter of one of Bonnie Prince Charlie's supporters, who had had his property confiscated by the government for his part in the 1745 rebellion.

In her will (1771) Sarah Hucks describes the

30. Portrait of Sarah Hucks (née Coghill) who inherited Wigbournes and changed its name to Aldenham House.

31. Robert Hucks, MP.

mansion as "Aldenham House, formerly called Wigbournes." In 1785, her son, Robert Hucks the younger, a brewer of Bloomsbury, made additions to the building, which included the library with the fine chimneypiece, and a Sansovino window (on the east side). A stone tablet in the courtyard describes his zeal: "These stables and improvements were begun and finish'd by Robert Hucks in the year 1785".

Robert Hucks did not marry and on his death in June, 1814, the house, together with properties in Clifton Hampden, went to two unmarried nieces, while Penne's Place had earlier been reduced to the status of a large farmhouse. However, Aldenham House was then left unoccupied by any of the family for many years, and was allowed to fall into a much neglected state until in 1841 both estates passed to a cousin, George Henry Gibbs, a senior partner of the banking house Antony Gibbs & Sons. He chose,

however, to live at Clifton Hampden, and Aldenham fell into an even more dilapidated state until his widow made it her home for some years after his death in Venice in 1842. Cussans, writing in 1881, says that "in 1846, the mother of the present owner came to live here, but at her death, in 1850, it remained unoccupied by the family until 1869, when Mr. Gibbs again came into residence. He thoroughly restored the old mansion, making many improvements, but in no way altering the character of the building. The Park, to which he has made some additions, now contains about two hundred acres."[2]

Henry Hucks Gibbs was ennobled in 1896 and took the name of Aldenham. He decided against much protest to alter the route of the Letchmore Heath to Elstree road which he felt passed too close to the house. In the process, he had the Wrestler's Inn demolished together with most of the medieval hamlet of Aldenham Wood. The

55.   Elstree Hall c. 1820, an early 16th-century building which stood slightly to the north-west of Schopwick Place. It was demolished in 1888.

pieces, one bearing the date 1529.' These were, it seems, removed to Hucks Gibbs' primary residence, Aldenham House, but a recent search at Aldenham House by the author and the Haberdashers' School archivist failed to find any trace of these. A more tangible reminder of the presence of the building remains in the form of a Tudor key found in the immediate vicinity of where the Hall once stood and is now in the possession of St. Nicholas Church. The Hall stood a few hundred yards to the north of Schopwick Place *(see below)*, and was possibly at one time the manor house.

SCHOPWICK PLACE

Schopwick Place stands in Elstree High Street about 300 yards north of the parish church. Replacing a Tudor building, it probably dates from 1722. It is now listed Grade II. The building has very recently been carefully restored and contains within its grounds the former site of Elstree Hall. A title deed which dates the very first building to the first quarter of the 16th century refers to the admission of "Thomas Roberts Gent. To Schopwicks within ye mannor of Tytburst at a Court Baron held there 25 June. 26 Hen.8.1528"

In 2002, whilst excavating to build a swimming

56.   Schopwick Place c. 1800

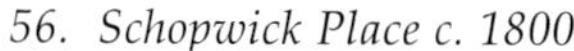

57. Schopwick Place 2006.

pool in the grounds, remains of a 19th-century pond belonging to Elstree Hall were unearthed.

Schopwick Place is now probably best known for being the former home of Sir Percy Everett, a friend of Lord Baden-Powell, founder of the Scout movement, with which Everett was also closely associated.[6]

The memoirs of Everett's daughter, Winn Everett, who died at the age of 95 in 1998 note that:

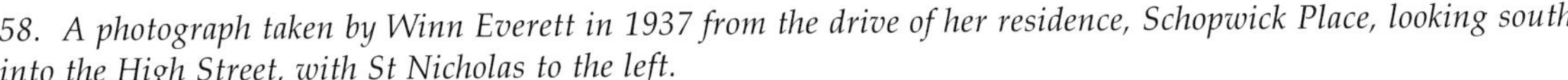

SIR PERCY EVERETT

Sir Percy Everett, Deputy Chief Scout since 1941, died on Saturday at his home in Hertfordshire, aged 81.

Percy Winn Everett was the second son of the late R. L. Everett. He was educated at Queen Elizabeth's School, Ipswich, and Trinity College, Cambridge, where he was a scholar and 15th Wrangler. He first met Baden-Powell at the home of Mr. C. Arthur (later Sir Arthur) Pearson in 1907, when Baden-Powell outlined his scheme for Scouting.

Everett was present at the experimental camps at Brownsea Island in 1907 and Humshaugh in 1908. He was County Commissioner for Hertfordshire, one of the first counties to be properly organized, from the beginning, and coupled with it the task of County Commissioner for Middlesex when that county was first organized. His services to the Boy Scouts Association included chairmanship of the headquarters general purposes committee and chairmanship of the finance committee. He was also Commissioner for Equipment. In 1917 he took on the work of treasurer of the Girl Guides Association. He was knighted in 1930, and four years later was appointed deputy Chief Commissioner. Everett was interested in hospital work, and was chairman of the Bushey and District and the Plaistow Maternity hospitals, and on the committee of the Royal Free Hospital, until the inauguration of the national health service.

59. An obituary to Sir Percy Everett in The Times *on 25 February 1952.*

58. A photograph taken by Winn Everett in 1937 from the drive of her residence, Schopwick Place, looking south into the High Street, with St Nicholas to the left.

'...we moved into Schopwick in 1921 because we knew the people living here and we all of us liked the house very much and when they were leaving, they said would you like it, I mean, would you like to buy it? We didn't have any agents or anything and we had a direct buy with Mr Kershaw's the owner. It was built in 1722, you know by the beading over the door. ....I came to Schopwick when I was 19. I was a student and I've been here ever since...'[7]

KENDAL'S, WATLING STREET, RADLETT
(now Radlett Preparatory School)

An older house was built by William Jephson, having purchased the estate from the sixth Earl of Salisbury in 1739. It takes its name from the Kendal family, the first recorded member being Jordan de Kendalle. It was Jephson's nephew Robert Phillimore who inherited the estate when Jephson, who is buried in Aldenham parish church, died in 1766. The building that now exists as Kendal's was built by Robert Phillimore during the latter part of the eighteenth century. The manor and house descended through four more generations of Phillimores until in 1887 Brough Phillimore died childless and the estate passed to a distant cousin, the first Baron Phillimore, a Lord of Appeal whose family seat was Shiplake, near Henley-on-Thames. He gave the manor of Titberst & Kendalls to his eldest son, Robert Charles Phillimore, referred to in local literature as 'Bobby'.

The breaking up of the estate as from 1898 led to the development of Radlett as we know it today, though the house survived.

Robert Phillimore died at an early age at Kendal's Hall in 1919. He predeceased his father and did not live to inherit the title.

For a period during the summer of 1904 Prince Louis of Battenberg (1854-1921)[8] rented Kendal's. The event is mentioned in Harold Knee's memoirs. He describes three shops which were situated in front of Radlett railway station. One of them, he tells us, belonged to the local barber, a Walter Massey:

60. *Walter George Frank Phillimore, 1st Baron Phillimore (1845-1929).*

"Walter Massey, a dapper little man with waxed moustaches, was the village barber and had his shop next to Mark Hall's (Mark Hall was the station master) ... on Walter's fascia board was written, PATRONISED BY HIS ROYAL HIGHNESS LOUIS OF BATTENBERG'. Prince Louis, father of the present Earl Mountbatten,[9] had stayed with his family at Kendal Hall for some months during the year 1904 and Walter had been his tonsorial artist and trimmed the royal beard etc."

The last Phillimore to live at Kendal's departed in 1926, and in 1980 it was acquired by Radlett Preparatory School.

RADNOR HALL

Radnor Hall, a seventeenth-century house, stood north-east of St Nicholas near Allum Lane, and was known for a long time as Palmers. By the 1930s it had become the Radnor Hall Country Club. The house was demolished in the 1950s and the Allum Lane rubbish tip now stands in its place.

RADLETT, HERTS.
THE KENDALLS ESTATE.

CONVEYANCES FREE OF LAW COSTS.   PAYMENTS SPREAD OVER 10 YEARS.

Particulars, Plan & Conditions of Sale

OF

FIFTY-EIGHT PLOTS

OF

FREEHOLD BUILDING LAND

FRONTING

Watling Street, the Main Road to Watford, Aldenham Avenue, and The Crosspath,

SUITABLE FOR THE ERECTION OF WELL-DESIGNED HOUSES
With Good Depths.

Adjoining Radlett Station on the Midland Railway and within easy distance of St. Albans.

EXCELLENT ROADS.   SEWERS LAID.   GOOD WATER SUPPLY.
TITHE FREE & FREE FROM LAND TAX.

Which will be Offered by Auction, by

MR. F. G. WHEATLEY,

IN CONJUNCTION WITH

MR. W. F. INGRAM,

IN A MARQUEE ON THE ESTATE.

NICOLL FARM

Nicoll Farm *(ill. 63)* lies on the north side of Allum Lane between Watling Street and Elstree and Boreham Wood Station. It is a timber-framed late medieval hall-house with a brick façade of *c.*1700, altered later. Of this building, Stephen Castle says that it is only one of two late medieval buildings to survive in Elstree parish: "It comprises a two bay open hall with queen-strut roof trusses and a two-storeyed service and solar at the west end. Adjoining the hall on the east side is a contemporary two-storeyed, two bay cross-wing, comprising a parlour on the ground floor and solar (chamber) on the first floor. This house dates from *c.*1500. A two-storeyed, two bay timber-framed extension was added on the west side of the building during the mid-17th century and includes a massive red brick chimney with diagonal stacks."[10]

61. The Kendal's estate in 1898, divided for sale into 58 plots.

62. A riding party at Radnor Hall in the 1930s.

78. *Barnet Lane at Woodcock Hill c.1904. This formed the boundary between Hertfordshire and Middlesex.*

79. *Shenley Road, looking east, 1903. Glenhaven House stood on the left.*

80. *Furze Hill looking towards Boreham Wood village, c. 1903.*

81. *Theobald Street, near the junction with Shenley Road, c. 1903, looking north.*

Some local features

WATLING STREET

Before the advent of modern government, the roads and lanes around Elstree, Boreham Wood, Radlett and Aldenham were narrow, pot holed, more often than not flooded, and in many instances subject to the attention of highwaymen. Watling Street, originally a Roman road, was narrow and overhung with forestry. We have a description from the antiquary William Stukeley in 1776 who followed the line of Watling Street identifying the Roman stations, and left us this account of late 18th-century Watling Street in the area:

> "Then by Colney-Street and Radway [Radlett]; thence almost disused, and scarce known but for its straitness: it continues direct but very narrow, the hedges having incroached upon it on both sides, till we arrive at our next station, *Suellaniacis*, upon Brockley hill, a little south of Elstree, and near Stanmore...."

HILL SLOUGH OR WEARE'S POND

Hill Slough achieved notoriety when in October of 1823 the slough, or pond featured in one of the nineteenth century's most 'popular' murders *(see p88)*. Harold Knee believes that the first mention of the slough was in the 'doubtful' charter of AD 785 when it was called Hilce Sloo. In 1513, in a licence granted by Sir Humphrey Coningsby, Hill Slough was referred to again as Hilleslowe. Situated on Tykeswater it was almost certainly seen as a land boundary.

Today, there is little to signify its presence as the pond was filled in during the early part of the twentieth century. But the site is accessible by footpath from Allum Lane, heading north parallel to Watling street, just where Tykeswater crosses the field, approximately 300 yards north of the junction with Allum Lane.

THEOBALD STREET

Theobald Street until well into the twentieth century was subject to flooding. That part of it which runs from Elstree through to Radlett

82. The water splash in Theobald Street.

known as the water splash lies just to the north of Rossington Avenue. A bridge was built in the 1920s to avoid the problem. Harold Knee recalls that "Theobald Street had at least three 'water splashes', or small streams, which crossed the road and, in abnormally wet weather, when the floods were out, children would hasten to the one between Tykes Water and Organ Hall Farm, take their stand on a high rickety foot-bridge, and watch cars and motor bikes endeavour to get through the swollen stream, and, to their huge delight, stall in the middle."

MEDBURN BRIDGE

Medburn Bridge, built in 1769, lay on Watling Street between Elstree and Radlett. It is mentioned in a letter dated 1825 from W.R. Phillimore, Lord of the Manor of Titburst and Kendals, and others, addressed to the magistrates. It states that the bridge was built by Phillimore's father and Mr Neate, the late Lord of the Manor of Aldenham. It had been "…erected … in great measure for their own convenience, the road being occasionally much overflowed and there previously as we are informed a mere hand-rail for foot passengers. Until lately there has been but little traffic over the bridge, comparatively speaking, but the greatly increased use of the road of late years by heavy wagons and stages, as well as for posting, has rendered the bridge dangerous, particularly since the formation of the reservoir on Aldenham Common, which produces an increased amount of water, particularly in winter, to such an extent that the arches…are not of sufficient size and strength to maintain…"

When the bridge was inspected in 1826 it was found to be extremely dangerous, the road being only 10' 6" wide in the centre, and the sides very low. The inspecting committee recommended that the width should be increased to 18'6" "which would allow the passage of stage coaches with much more ease." The bridge was rebuilt by the County, and a Herts Session Roll reports that "a stage-coach now passes and re-passes it daily, and the road has otherwise become one of considerable traffic and importance."

Getting About

FOUL WINE AND PERT CHAMBERMAIDS

Elstree, on a main arterial route, was well provided with stage coaches leaving London to various parts of the country. But these were generally uncomfortable and not the romantic vehicles we imagine. John Byng, 5th Viscount Torrington observed in 1781 that

> "the imposition in travelling is abominable; the innkeepers are insolent, the hostlers are sulky, the chambermaids are pert, and the waiters are impertinent; the meat is tough, the wine is foul, the beer is hard, the sheets are wet, the linen dirty, and the knives are never cleaned."[1]

An 1832 directory provides a summary of coach services five years before Victoria came to the throne:

> "TO LONDON, the *Self Defence* (from St.Albans), calls at the Green Dragon, and the *Accommodation* calls at the Plough [now The East Chinese Restaurant!], every morning (Sunday excepted) at nine – the *Safety*, calls at the same Inn, every morning (Sunday excepted) at eight – the *Crown Prince* (from Birmingham), calls at the Artichoke, every morning (Sun. excepted) at half-past eight – and a coach (from Shenley), calls at the Red Lion, every morn at ½ past 8; all go thro' Edgeware.
> TO BIRMINGHAM, the *Crown Prince* (from London), calls at the Artichoke, every evening at seven; goes through St.Albans, Redburn, Dunstable, Stoney Stratford, Daventry, Leamington, &c.
> TO ST.ALBANS, the *Safety* (from London), calls at the Plough, every afternoon at four, and the *Accommodation*, every evening at six – and the *Self Defence*, calls at the Green Dragon, every afternoon at five.
> TO SHENLEY, a coach (from London), calls at the Red Lion, every even."

However, the roads were often flooded and potholed and there are numerous accounts of coach accidents in the Elstree area. One in *The Times* of February 1819 refers to the death of Henry Harper Crewe which occurred when a wheel of his carriage struck one of the posts at the gateway of a cottage near his house at Boreham Wood.

Much later another unfortunate accident is reported in *The Times* of 31st October 1905,

83. Elstree and Boreham Wood station. The station master's house to the left still stands. To the right is the entrance to the brickworks.

involving 'Mr Justice and Lady Phillimore' who were injured while driving to church at Elstree. His injuries were mild but hers severe, but she recovered in a fortnight while staying at her son's house, Kendals (see p50).

THE RAILWAY ARRIVES

The Midland Railway Company, rather late in contriving a London terminus, commenced work at Elstree, digging a tunnel to extend its line from Bedford in 1865, eventually to finish at St Pancras. Elstree station opened on 13 July 1868, with 6 trains each week day, travelling in each direction. The line also connected Elstree to St Albans and Luton in the north.

Apart from the stationmaster's house in Allum Lane, which dates from around 1867-1868, the present station bears little relation to the first building.

A MISDIRECTED TRAIN: ELSTREE'S FIRST ACCIDENT

It was only a matter of a few years before two accidents in rapid succession occurred at Elstree. The first was on 22 July 1874 at Elstree Station: *The Times* report of the 22nd September 1874 reads as follows:

"…an excursion train of school children, due to leave Elstree for Haverstock-hill at 9pm., was starting from a siding on the back or east side of the up-platform, when, in consequence of a pair of points having been set in the wrong direction, the engine ran into a mound of earth at the end of the siding instead of going out on to the main line. Four adult passengers and 16 children have complained of injury. None of the company's servants were injured. The collision has occurred in consequence of the forgetfulness of the station porter, who ought to have opened the points near the south end of the siding to allow the train to run on the main line, but who forgot the necessity for doing so, and left them open for the dead end of the siding: and this man appears fully to have admitted his forgetfulness."

The July accident was a harbinger for something much more serious: *The Times* on 9

EASTER HOLIDAY.

COOK'S

HALF-DAY EXCURSION

TO

ELSTREE, RADLETT, ST. ALBANS HARPENDEN & LUTON,

On MONDAY, APRIL 21st, 1924

WILL RUN AS UNDER:

FROM	Times of starting	RETURN FARES—THIRD CLASS				
		To Elstree	To Radlett	To St. Albans	To Harpenden	To Luton
	p.m.	s. d.	s. d.	s. d.	s. d.	s. d.
ST. PANCRAS	12.35	1 7	1 11	2 6	3 1	3 9
Kentish Town ...	12.42	1 5	1 8	2 4	2 11	3 7
Finchley Road ...	12.48	1 2	1 6	2 1	2 8	3 5
West Hampstead ...	12.52	1 1	1 6	2 0	2 7	3 4
Cricklewood ...	12.56	1 0	1 3	1 10	2 5	3 2
Hendon ...	1.2	0 9	1 0	1 8	2 2	2 11
Mill Hill ...	1.8	0 5	0 9	1 4	1 11	2 8
Elstree ...	1.15	—	0 5	1 0	1 6	2 3
Radlett ...	1.20	—	—	0 7	1 3	1 11

RETURN ARRANGEMENTS. PASSENGERS MUST RETURN SAME DAY AS UNDER
From Luton at 7.40 p.m.; Harpenden at 7.53 p.m.; St. Albans at 8.5 p.m.
Radlett at 8.13 p.m.; Elstree at 8.21 p.m.

PASSENGERS ARE REQUESTED TO OBTAIN TICKETS IN ADVANCE.
Tickets can be purchased at the "MIDLAND" STATIONS, and Offices of
THOS. COOK & SON.

CONDITIONS OF ISSUE OF TICKETS.

CHILDREN under three years of age, free; three years and under twelve, half-fares.
NOTICE.—The tickets are not transferable, and will be available on the date of issue only, by the trains, and at the stations named; if used on any other date, by any other train, or at any other station than those named, the tickets will be forfeited and the full ordinary fare charged.
The Company give notice that tickets for this excursion are issued at a reduced rate, and subject to the condition that the Company shall not be liable for any loss, damage, injury, or delay to passengers arising from any cause whatsoever.
No luggage allowed.
Should the Company consider it necessary or desirable, from any cause, to alter or cancel these arrangements, they reserve to themselves the right to do so.

March, 1924.   **H. G. BURGESS, General Manager.**

B 18/24E.   Thos. Cook & Son, Print &c., Ludgate Circus, London, E.C.4.

84. As late as 1924 places such as Elstree and Luton were thought of as Easter excursion locations.

November 1874 reported:

"A terrible accident, resulting in the death of one passenger and the serious injury of several others, occurred near the Elstree and Boreham-wood station, on the Midland Railway, at a few minutes before 7 o'clock on Saturday evening. The Midland Manchester express, leaving that place at 1 p.m., and timed to reach St. Pancras at 6 40 p.m., consisted of an engine and tender, brake-van, and half-a-dozen carriages, made up of composite and third-class coaches. The train passed St. Alban's at its accustomed speed, and, not being timed to stop before reaching London, ran through Elstree and Boreham-wood

93. *The former National School in Elstree. It is now a synagogue.*

94. *Elstree Preparatory School at Hill House on Elstree Hill South, in 1903. It is a graceful red brick house built for John Rudge in 1779, and was used as a school for boys at least from 1847 until 1939.*

95. Hill House, now a nursing home. The essential features of the building have been preserved, as has the tree standing in front of the entrance drive 103 years after Illustration 94 was taken.

Still "No Sale" for Elstree Chapel

May be Used for Lectures

"FOR SALE" reads the notice near the chapel in Elstree High-street. This chapel, which is over 200 years old, is up for sale because its owners, the S.O.S. Society, have no further use for it as a chapel.

The chapel was, for many years, before the war, used by the pupils of Elstree Preparatory School, which is now known as Hill House and is occupied by the S.O.S. Society.

The pupils of the school used to attend services at the chapel regularly by using a tunnel running under Elstree High-street. Since the beginning of the war, when the Army took over the school, the chapel has not been in use.

A spokesman of the estate agents acting for the S.O.S. Society told the *Post* on Tuesday: "We have been in touch with other churches regarding the sale of the chapel, but our inquiries have not been successful. However, one religious body has shown interest in buying it."

The spokesman stated that if the chapel were sold to this group it would be used for lectures and not religious purposes. The sports ground adjoining the chapel, he said, would not be included in the sale. It is used by the Mill Hill Rugby Football Club who have a yearly tenancy, and it is zoned as open space on the town map.

He stated that the sale of the chapel was made difficult by the fact that its use is restricted by deeds and the fact that people are buried in the grounds.

96. The chapel belonging to the Elstree Preparatory School was difficult to sell because it had interments. Eventually the burials were exhumed and reburied in St Nicholas churchyard., but the chapel was demolished.

respectively, at Hatcham. This arrangement then changed when two new schools were built – one for boys at Hampstead, the other for girls at Acton. The boys moved out of Hampstead in 1961 to Aldenham House, Elstree (their old building is now Hampstead Comprehensive) and in 1974 the girls moved from Acton to a site at Elstree near to Aldenham House.

The two schools (*see illustrations on pp 31-42*) now occupy grounds and playing fields covering approximately 104 acres bounded by Butterfly Lane, and Aldenham Road.

Notable *alumni* include the comedian David Baddiel, Leon Brittan politician, the historian Simon Schama, Nicholas Serota director of Tate Modern, Sir Martin Sorrell, advertising guru and the broadcaster Alan Whicker.

ALDENHAM SCHOOL

Aldenham school was founded by Richard Platt in 1596, proprietor of the Old Swan Brewery in the City of London, who had been Master of the Brewers' Company in 1576 and 1581. After his death the Brewers' Company became responsible for the school's management.

The foundation stone was laid in 1597, though it could not be said that Platt had chosen an ideal location, since there were few local pupils. In effect, just as at Highgate School, it was a village elementary school at which the Master was permitted to take in paying pupils to eke out his salary.

Many such grammar schools received an investigation and renovation during the 19th century to counteract the neglect of those supposedly administering old bequests. Oddly enough, Aldenham was again in tandem with Highgate School which too remained fairly moribund until the appointment of a zealous headmaster. In the case of Aldenham it was the Rev. Alfred Leeman who established the academic credentials so sadly lacking before.

98. Richard Platt, from a portrait dated 1600, when he was 76.

97. Richard Platt's original school building, completed in 1599, and demolished in 1825. From an engraving dated 1825.

Then there was a financial windfall when Platt's old estate at St Pancras, a slummy area at Somers Town, was bought up by the Midland Railway to establish St Pancras station. (Aldenham Street exists today north of the British Library which, too, is on former Platt estate land.)

Between 1877 and 1899 the school grew from 47 pupils to 175 and there was a major building programme, though it still retains some of its Tudor buildings.

Alumni include the broadcasters Jack de Manio and Dale Winton and the sculptor Sir Alfred Gilbert who designed the Eros statue in Piccadilly Circus.

In 1878, while excavations were being made for the construction of a swimming bath on the north side of the school, workmen came upon a large quantity of broken Roman tiles and pottery, at a depth of four or five feet from the surface. It is supposed that there was a pottery factory close by.

BOREHAM WOOD'S FIRST SCHOOL

Boreham Wood's first school came into being c.1870 at 35 Theobald Street, but its existence is a bit of a mystery. Its building still stands and is used for a working men's club. In 1872 the Ordnance Survey identified the building as a school converted from a religious meeting house. Lesley Davies of the Elstree & Boreham Wood Museum, who has researched the history of Elstree and Boreham Wood schools, observes that the only identification of its existence as a school is on that map, and on the OS map of 1898 the building is a mission hall. As a new purpose built school was established a few yards away in 1896 it can be assumed that the children were moved there from the earlier building.

The new building was tucked away in an alley which is almost opposite the Wellington pub in Theobald Street. This is now known as 27a Theobald Street and is barely recognisable in its dilapidated state and is unlisted.

Davies tells us that the school took up to 66 infants while children over 7 went to the Elstree National School. According to a former pupil, William Brooks, there were two classes, a 1st

99. *Boreham Wood's first school, in a religious meeting house by c. 1870. The building survives as a working men's club.*

100. *Boreham Wood's first purpose-built school in Theobald Street, as from 1896.*

and 2nd year with each having 25 children. There was just one room with a screen in the middle between the classes.

Kelly's Directory of 1898 quotes an average attendance of 51, but in 1912 this was down to 43. By 1917, with the rapid population growth of Elstree and Boreham Wood the school was closed down and the pupils transferred to Furzehill County Mixed School or Elstree Church of England School.

MEDBURN SCHOOL

This was situated on the west side of Watling Street, a few hundred yards north of the present day junction with Butterfly Lane. It operated from 1864 to 1950 serving the children of poor

101. *Pupils at the National School for infants in Theobald Street in 1908. The headmistress (left) is Mrs Downing. The boy standing next to her is William Brooks - future author of books on the area.*

families within the parish of Aldenham - boys from Elstree and Boreham Wood attended. Donald Wratten tells us that about 100 boys of all ages were taught in a single classroom, later subdivided by a wooden partition, by a headmaster and his two or three assistants. A house for the headmaster formed an integral part of the school. Harold Knee, a one time resident of Radlett, was a pupil there between 1905 and 1909. He writes, "We were a pretty ragged-looking lot. The majority of boys wore patched clothing, had only one pair of boots to their name, and almost invariably had nits in their hair…fleas abounded and could be picked up almost anywhere….sanitation was still pretty crude and earth closets there were in plenty. But although there were rags, hardship and distress and quite a number of families were below the poverty line, the majority of children were fed on

102. *The original Medburn School dating from c. 1860. It survives just north of the junction of Watling Street and Butterfly Lane.*

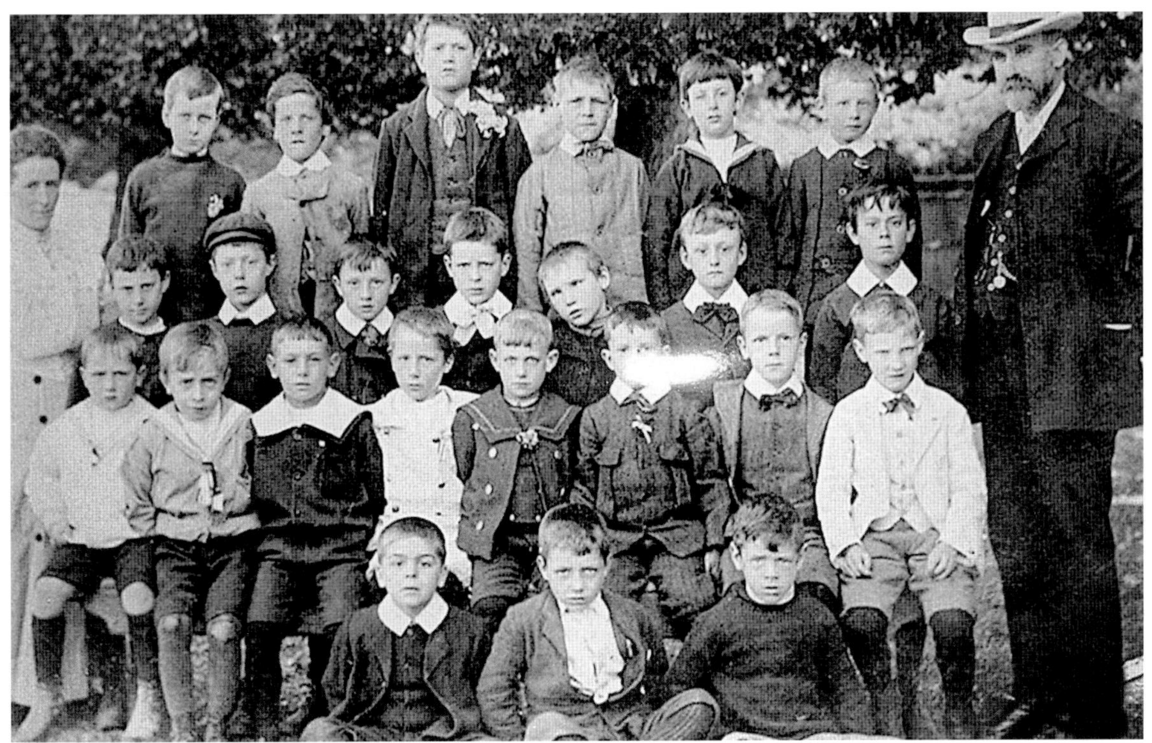

103. Some pupils at Medburn School in the early 20th century. There is not a single smile in the entire picture. It is likely that the gentleman on the right was the head, Frederick J. Forfeitt, who retired in 1922, both feared and respected by the children.

good, plain, honest grub."

Medburn was funded by the charitable trustees of the Platts estate. The building is still there and is now the Medburn Kennels and Cattery.

FURZE HILL SCHOOL

Furze Hill School opened on 12 August 1912 and was Boreham Wood's first county council school. It is a reflection of the rapid growth taking place in Boreham Wood that in 1912 there were 223 pupils, increasing to 400 the following year. The school burned down in 1949 and reopened in 1950. It subsequently underwent a number of name changes and closed down altogether on 20 July 2001.

HILLSIDE BOARDING SCHOOL

This boarding school in Allum Lane occupied what previously was called Barham House *(see p43)*. Lesley Davies records that in the 1881 census the school had about 50 pupils, probably all boarders as their home addresses included the West Indies and Plymouth. They were all boys with the exception of 4 girls who were the proprietor's children. The school is last recorded in *Kelly's Directory* in 1882.

1   I am indebted to Lesley Davies of the Elstree and Boreham Wood Museum for her extensive assistance in compiling the section on education.

Looking after the Poor

ALMSHOUSES

The almshouses in Elstree, founded and endowed by George Byng in 1840, stood just to the south of the Artichoke public house in Elstree Hill North. There were three under one roof. A woodcut from 1824 shows them standing in the position described. The almshouses and the old school building adjacent (which dated from *c.* 1814 – *see Learning Places*) were demolished by Henry Hucks Gibbs of Aldenham House. He built cottages for his estate workers on the site, which still stand, just to the south of the Artichoke. Then, in 1883 Hucks Gibbs built Nos 1-3 The Almshouses between New Road and the new National School. These replaced the almshouses on Elstree Hill North.

THE FEMALE ORPHANS' HOME

Walford, writing in 1883, notes that "close by the church was established, about a quarter of a century ago, an institution which in its time has done much good work – namely, the Female Orphans' Home, a charity which has since been transferred to Tangley Park, near Hampton Court. This Home had a very humble origin. Towards the close of the year 1855, a private gentleman, not rich in broad acres or in stores of gold and silver, but pursuing his business as an accountant in the City, resolved to open a 'home for destitute orphan girls'. He was living with his mother in a pleasant London suburb, when a little girl was left wholly destitute, her father and mother having perished by the cholera..."[1] The enterprise was a resounding success with further homes being opened in other areas in London and the surrounding country.

104. On the left is the National School. To the right, the small cottage-like buildings are the almshouses built in 1883 by Hucks Gibbs. Photo 2006.

THE WORKHOUSE

Workhouses were designed to be unpleasant.

"...it was distinctly laid down as a truth, incontrovertible in principle and sanctioned by experience that subsistence in a Workhouse must be made less desirable to the recipient than subsistence obtained by independent exertion. That the confinement, frugal fare, strict discipline, seclusion and other irksome circumstances attending an abode within a Workhouse should be so enforced as to deter the idle, the dissolute, the worthless, and such like Applicants for admission, the dread of being driven to shelter within its walls thus serving as a stimulant to exertion and to the observance of thrifty and provident habits."[2]

The workhouse for Elstree and Boreham Wood was that built for the Barnet Union, in which they were a constituent. Built for 150-200 people, it was situated on Barnet Common and opened in the spring of 1837. Benjamin Woodcock, Master of the Barnet Union Workhouse, kept a diary which covers the period from September 1836 to May 1838. It is a sobering insight into the business of survival in early 19th-century Hertfordshire and Middlesex, as well as a reminder of the gulf that existed between the haves and have nots. Within the diary are a number of entries relating to the unfortunates from Elstree forced to seek shelter in the workhouse.

"18 September 1836: Admitted by order of R Officer, John Williams and his wife Elizabeth paupers of Elstree, both of which was in a state of intoxication. The Woman who was certainly the worst of the two, was very pert."

The next series of entries are intriguing in that it leaves one wondering what became of the 'woman Trott' and her baby:

"Saturday June 3rd: Eliza Trott aged 18, Pauper from Elstree, was admitted in the house by an order of removal dated 9th May on Saturday 3 June. The Medical Officer pronounced her to be in a forward state of Pregnancy. This Girl who within 2 months of her confinement has not reached 18 years, & brought up to the Methodist Chapel.

Saturday August 5th. Eliza Trott, Pauper of Elstree, was delivered of a Male infant in the workhouse on Saturday 5 August about 6 o'clock evening, both of which are doing well.

Thursday September 21st 1837. The Medical Officer attended at the Workhouse on Tuesday 26 & Vaccinated all the young Children except the infant Trott whose Mother objected.

Thursday November 23rd 1837. Eliza Trott went up to London early on Monday Morning after the situation as Wet Nurse, but the Lady had engaged with a person on Saturday. She paid her expenses.

Thursday November 30th. Francis Young from Hadley called at the Workhouse on Monday to see Eliza Trott and Persuaded her to go out of the house. The following morning Eliza Trott gave the usual Notice & was discharged. Eliza Trott went out."

At this point Eliza Trott and her infant disappear from history. It is apparent from the next entry that the workhouse was seen by others as a source of cheap labour:

"Thursday February 8th 1838: Mrs Melville, Boreham Wood, applied at the Workhouse on Monday afternoon for a servant Girl. She saw Georgiana Hawkins, Pauper of Ridge, & engaged with her to go on Wednesday.

Thursday February 15th 1838: Georgina Hawkins aged 16, Pauper of Ridge, was discharged from the house on Thursday 15 February. Gone as Menial Servant to Mrs Melville, Boreham Wood."

The 1792 vestry records for Elstree tell us that

"Mr.Wm.Tanner agreed to take into his service Rebecca Cook, aged 10 years, and to supply her with proper food and clothing. The Parish agreeing to cloath her properly at first, and to allow W.Tanner 2/6 per week in consideration of his taking and keeping the said Rebeca Cook."

Canon Eales, referring to this particular entry, says that "there was something to be said for the custom of apprenticing an orphan or deserted child to domestic service instead of sending it to the poorhouse. In practice the child became one of the family."

The Master also recorded some more cheerful details. On Christmas Day 1837 "the inmates had all plenty of Roast Beef and Plum Pudding and was very comfortable except the Cook who got intoxicated soon after Dinner. We sent her to Bed." Much later, to celebrate Victoria's jubilee all the men were given beer and tobacco, the women new petticoats and the children toys and sweets.

The Workhouse closed in 1839, but its infirmary survived to become the core of Barnet General Hospital.

CHARITY

There were a number of local charities, which are listed in the *Victoria County History of Hertfordshire* relating to this area. The earliest dates from 1616, when Robert Briscoe left 6 acres of land to bring in an income of £2 to be given to the poor and £1 to the repair of the parish church. Similarly, in 1726 John Warren left a similar arrangement which also provided £2 annually to the poor as did Robert Warren, his brother, in 1730. He also left money to apprentice a poor child.

The Elstree parish registers record that alms were collected for a number of purposes. Some of the most interesting include an entry in 1670 for redeeming English captives in slavery under the Turk. The amount raised was £3 9s. 6d. Two years later money was collected for the redemption of Michaell and Peter Kys, Hungarians.

At a vestry meeting in 1803 "... it was resolved that money be raised and laid out weekly in the purchase of flour, oatmeal, herrings, potatoes, rice, and other articles of provision, and sent to some convenient place in the parish to be dealt out amongst the poor inhabitants of the parish at one half of the prime cost in proportion to the number of persons in each family."

1   Edward Walford, *Greater London* (1883), p304.
2   Poor Law administrators in 1834, cited in *Down and Out in Hertfordshire*, a symposium on the old and new Poor Law by Gutchen, Truwert and Peters, p9.

Crimes and Punishments

There are illustrations of St Nicholas Church showing the parish lock-up or cage, which stood at the north-west corner of the churchyard, almost fronting Watling Street to the right of the lych-gate. An entry in the Vestry minutes for 1792 records:

> "That a new trunk be put down instead of the footbridge in the second field in the Church Path, and that a Cage be built for the use of the Parish 6 feet square inside, all of oak, boarded round about 3ft: 4 inc: from the ground: to iron the insides of the bars, and put a good lock and hinges on the door for the sum of 3 guineas."

A cage was used to detain criminals thought to be guilty of relatively minor offences, until they could be dealt with by the local magistrates

The early site of the local gallows was at the appropriately named High Cross on the Watford Road, mid way between Aldenham church and Radlett. The manor of Aldenham was in the possession of the abbey of St. Albans until the time of the Dissolution under Henry VIII, although there had been a dispute, dating to 1249, between St Albans and Westminster Abbey as to the manor's ownership *(see p12)*. At that time, because of the dispute, it was agreed "that the gallows erected in a place called Keneprowe, should be in common to both Abbots, on which to hang persons condemned to death in the Court of Aldenham." ('Keneprow' was at High Cross.)

A man suspended by the neck was supposed to be a wholesome moral lesson to his former associates. The abbots therefore acted wisely in their selection of Keneprow; for on its elevated site, the result of unlawfully taking fish from the

105. A detail of Illustration 6, showing the stocks outside St Nicholas church at the end of the 18th century.

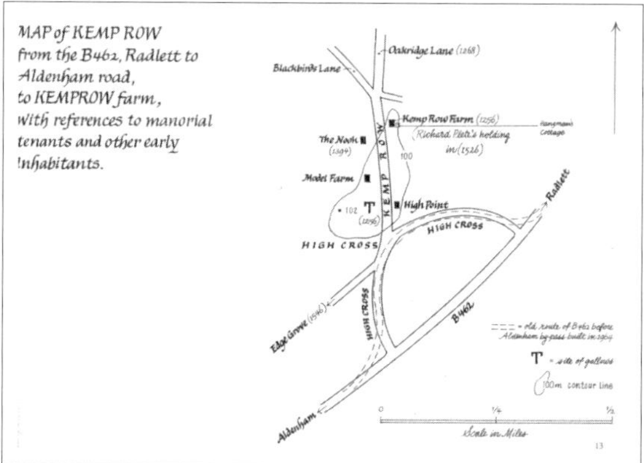

106. *The Hangman's Cottage, now incorporated into Kemp Row Farm. The structure of the room, originally the cottage, has many Tudor beams and bricks including two doors which stand barely five feet high.*

107. *Map of the probable site of the gallows, marked T in the grounds of Model Farm. Drawn by David Robertson.*

abbatial waters could be plainly seen by the men of both Aldenham and St Albans.'[1] The gallows were erected round about 1256, and remained for around 200 years.

David Robertson in his book on the manor of Aldenham, took some trouble in establishing exactly where the gallows were sited. There are a number of clues, and the most likely location is on the land of Model Farm where the tower of St. Albans abbey is clearly to be seen. Intriguingly there is a lean-to building at the back of Kemp Row Farm on the opposite side of the road to where the gallows stood which has traditionally been known as the hangman's cottage.

CRIME COMES EARLY TO BOREHAM WOOD

Cussans writing in 1881 relates what is probably the first recorded crime in Boreham Wood, dating from the 13th century when he says "… John le

108. Kemprow. Model Farm on the right is the presumed site of the gallows. This is the highest point of the area, at 340 feet, with a direct view to St Albans five miles away.

Irisshe, and others, killed, and cut off the head of Robert de Holand, near Boreham Wood." Beyond this statement we are left to speculate as to the reason for this extreme murder.

The early Court Rolls for Aldenham contain everyday crimes and misdemeanours in the parish. They include minor offences such as selling ale not up to strength, for which the vendors were fined. Stage-coach drivers were not popular and there are numerous records of fines imposed on the drivers for dangerous driving and overcrowding. One such example appeared in *The Times* of 21 August 1818, when seven owners of various coaches were fined a total of £510 for carrying more passengers than Parliament allowed.

The theft of lead from the roof of St. Nicholas occurred in both 1803 and in 1837. There is no record of anyone being apprehended for the 1803 crime, but in 1837 William Hughes and some associates were charged with the offence and the parish was presented with a number of bills by people who had successfully brought the thieves to justice and for the replacement of the lead:

"Mr Franklin's bill for Humphrey and Lowe prosecuted and convicted of stealing Lead from the church, and for endeavouring to capture Wm.Hughes   £23. 4. 8
Reward to Isaac Pye and George Wardle, officers of the Barnet Association, for capturing the above   £10.10
Mr. Franklin's bill for the prosecution and conviction of James Chalmers and John Chapman   £17.17.10
Mr. Bodimeade's bill for replacing the Lead stolen
Debit: £22. 10. 0
Credit for old Lead   £18.   10. 6
Difference £3. 19. 6

EXTENSIVE DEPRADATION

In *The Times* of 15 November, 1823:

"The neighbourhood of Elstree, on the borders of Hertfordshire, has not only been rendered remarkable by the discovery of the perpetrators of a most atrocious murder committed there, but also, within a few days, by the detection of part of a gang of extensive and systematic plunderers, who have for many months infested that part of the country. During the whole of the last winter, and up to the present time, scarcely

109. *The court room in Aldenham House where magistrates presided during the latter part of the 19th century.*

a night has elapsed that some stable, coach-house, larder, or fowl-house, has not been broken into and property of all descriptions contained in such places carried off to a vast extent. Indeed, to such a height had this evil grown, that it became quite unsafe for any gentleman residing about Elstree, Boreham-wood, Stanmore, Edgeware &c.,to leave any property in their out-houses during the night: and all the activity of the magistrates had hitherto failed to detect, or put a stop to the proceedings of these plunderers...."

Another article from *The Times* of 17 July 1840 is headed ROBBERY AND OUTRAGE ON A LADY, and tells us:

"About noon on Saturday last a lady named Harris, an inhabitant of Elstree, who is of an exceedingly nervous temperament, while walking along the high road, in the vicinity of her residence, found herself suddenly in the midst of a horde of Irish labourers (about 30 or 40), who were on the tramp, who importuned her for alms, which she declined giving them, having only half-a-sovereign in her purse. Having with difficulty freed herself from them, and proceeded a short distance along the road, she, from the excitement she laboured under from the importunity of the beggars, swooned away, in which state she was found by a tradesman in the neighbourhood, who was driving that way in his cart, who instantly jumped out to her assistance, and, on her reviving, offered his services to see her to her residence. Mrs Harris, however, unfortunately declined his offer, saying she felt better, and should be able to reach home without assistance. She then proceeded on her way, but the individual before mentioned, suddenly missing her from the road, returned to look after her, when, not being able to find her, he went to the house of a gentleman named Carter, near the spot, and informed the servants of the state in which he had found Mrs. Harris, and of his having suddenly lost sight of her, requesting them to see after her. One of the servants accordingly went in search of her, when hearing her screams, proceeding into a plantation at the side of the road, he observed at a short distance the unfortunate lady on the ground, and a ruffian standing over. On seeing the servant approaching the fellow ran away and effected his escape. On reaching Mrs. Harris she was found to be in a state of insensibility; and, assistance being procured, she was carried to the house of Mr. Carter, and from there in her own carriage to the residence of her husband, where she received every medical attention her distressing state demanded."

Her 'ruffian' was arrested, fined £5 for common assault and in default of payment committed to hard labour for two months.

MARTHA RAY

Martha Ray was born in Elstree in 1746, the daughter of a local labourer. She was apprenticed to a milliner in Clerkenwell, but at the age of sixteen she became a singer at the Covent Garden Theatre, where she caught the attention of the Earl of Sandwich. Cussans relates the events as follows:

"James Hackman was a mercer's apprentice of Gosport, but having been left a legacy of some amount, he persuaded his parents to buy him an Ensigncy in the 68th Foot. When quartered at Huntingdon, he was invited to Hinchinbroke, where he met Martha Ray, a lady of an elegant person, great sweetness of manners, and of a remarkable judgment and execution in vocal and instrumental music.

It is unnecessary to recount the wretched details which followed. Hackman, still infatuated with the frail Beauty, who had borne several children to Lord Sandwich, took holy orders, and begged her to marry him. She refused, and one night, as she was leaving the theatre, accompanied by Lord Coleraine and an Italian singer – Signora Galli – maddened, as he said, by the linkman calling for Lady Sandwich's coach, Hackman shot her through the head, using one of her love-letters for the wad. He then unsuccessfully attempted to shoot himself, and both falling to the ground together, were taken to the Shakespeare Tavern."[2]

This murder took place on 14th April 1779, and Hackman was executed, after due trial at the Old Bailey, five days later at Tyburn. He "evinced [a] most perfect resignation to his fate, united

110. Martha Ray and the 4th Earl of Sandwich.

111. Martha Ray's burial place in St Nicholas churchyard.

with the settled composure of a man that felt he had survived everything that was dear to him."

Martha Ray was buried in St Nicholas Church, Elstree in a vault next to her mother. In 1820 the coffin containing her embalmed and perfectly preserved body was discovered by workmen under a pew and moved to a position under the chancel. She remained there until 1824 when she resumed her post-mortem travels to find a final resting place in an unmarked grave in the churchyard.

In 1920, the then Earl of Sandwich had a tombstone erected over her grave.

THE ELSTREE MURDER

The 'Elstree Murder' of 1823 was one of the most prominent and eagerly followed murders of the nineteenth century. It took place in Radlett, but the unfortunate William Weare, the victim, had his body thrown into a pond, Hill Slough, which lay within 300 yards of the corner of Allum Lane and Watling Street in Elstree. Upon its recovery, the body was taken to the Artichoke public house, about half a mile to the north on Elstree Hill North, and the subsequent inquest took place there.

The suspect, John Thurtell, was born in 1794, the son of the then mayor of Norwich. A fairly wealthy young man and a gambler, he had a grudge against a fellow gambler, solicitor William Weare, whom he accused of having cheated him of £300 in a game of cards and to whom he now owed, by the standards of the day, this vast sum. Thurtell's lifestyle involved prizefighting, gambling, insurance fraud. His companions, Probert and Hunt, who were accomplices in the murder, had equally disparate lifestyles.

Probert had a lease on a small farmhouse in Gills Hill Lane, Radlett from where it was rumoured he was operating an illegal distillery. He invited Weare to spend a weekend gambling and hunting with him and some friends at the cottage . They travelled up from London along Watling Street together in Thurtell's gig on 24 October 1823. Hunt travelled separately behind, stopping at a number of inns, so thus was not present at the murder. As they neared the cottage Thurtell confronted Weare over his behaviour.

He drew a pistol and fired its single shot at Weare's face, the bullet glancing off his cheekbone as the gun had misfired. Weare leapt from the gig offering to trade the £300 for his life. Thurtell overpowered him, and as shooting had not worked Thurtell set about the now dazed Weare with a penknife and cut his throat. He also rammed the muzzle of the gun into Weare's skull with maximum force, leaving blood, hair and tissue in the barrel.

Probert and Hunt, helped Thurtell dispose of Weare's body. Initially they put it into a pond in the garden of Probert's cottage but later, under cover of darkness moved it and threw it into another pond in Elstree, Hill Slough, near the corner of Allum Lane and Watling Street. The following day Thurtell and Hunt returned to the scene of the murder in order to locate the murder weapons. They were spotted by two workmen who found the gun and handed it over to a farmer, Charles Nichols who in turn handed it to the Watford magistrates.

A murder investigation began. As the owner of the cottage, Probert was the first to be questioned and realising his predicament turned King's Evidence. Following the interrogation of witnesses, and despite the lack of a body Thurtell, Hunt, and Probert were arrested. Weare had by then been reported by friends as missing. Hunt appeared to the magistrates as the weak point, and in return for a promise that his life would be spared, he revealed the location of the body. On 30th October it was exhumed from Hill Slough, and on 31st October an inquest was held at the nearby Artichoke.

Thurtell and Hunt were taken into custody and came up for trial at the January sitting of the Hertford Assizes before Mr Justice Park. Thurtell was charged with the murder and Hunt with being an accessory. It was virtually impossible for them to get a fair trial for two reasons. Firstly their guilt was seen as self-evident by both the press and the public, to the extent that the judge remarked that if "these statements of evidence before trial which corrupt the purity of the administration of justice in its source are not checked, I tremble for the fate of our country."

The newspapers showed great interest in Thurtell's case and every detail was lapped up by an eager public. It was to be the last trial in England conducted under the 16th-century principle in which the accused had to defend himself against the prosecution, being allowed only to make a speech after the evidence against them had been heard and not being allowed to cross examine the prosecution witnesses. This was hardly conducive to a fair trial and neither man was represented by counsel. Thurtell made a lengthy and somewhat rambling address to the court in which he tried to shift the blame for the killing to Probert. He referred to his Christian upbringing and also made references, apparently, to Voltaire and Saint Paul, all of which failed to impress either the judge or the jury. A character witness said of Thurtell, "I always thought him a respectable man." Being asked by the judge what he meant by this he replied, "He kept a gig." This was not in itself enough to save him and it took the jury just twenty minutes to find both accused guilty. Mr. Justice Park then sentenced them to death and

ordered that Thurtell's body be sent to anatomists after execution.

Hunt's sentence was commuted to transportation for life and he was duly shipped to Australia's Botany Bay where he was to live on for very many years.

NEW GALLOWS

Thurtell was returned to Hertford prison to await execution. He had the dubious privilege of a second claim to fame. He was executed at Hertford Gaol on a new form of gallows which incorporated a proper drop, specially built for him. This design did away with the need for ladders and carts to get the prisoner suspended and was copied for several other prisons round the country, becoming effectively the standard pattern of its day. A very similar one was used at York Castle from the mid 1820s. Construction began before the trial, so certain was everybody of the outcome! Mr. Nicholson, the Under Sheriff of Hertfordshire supervised the work and the gallows consisted of a "temporary platform with a falling leaf (single trap door) supported by bolts which could be withdrawn in an instant" so launching the criminal into eternity, as was the contemporary expression. The substantial cross beam was supported by two equally substantial uprights, about 8 feet high. The enclosure beneath the beam consisted of boards 7 feet high and dovetailed into each other so that there were no gaps (through which the body could be viewed). It was 30 feet long and 15 feet deep with a short flight of steps up to the platform at the back leading directly from the prison door. The whole gallows was painted black and presented "a very gloomy appearance". The walls of the platform rose approximately 2 feet above the platform so the bulk of the prisoner's body was hidden from view after the drop. The outer enclosure was for the javelin men who stood guard at hangings to prevent escape or rescue attempts.

James Foxen, was the hangman. Thurtell dressed for the occasion and was described as being "elegantly attired in a brown great coat with a black velvet collar, light breeches and

112. The execution of John Thurtell at Hertford gaol on 9 January 1824. 15,000 people attended. Thurtell was one of the first to be executed on the new gallows which operated by a drop mechanism.

113. The burial of Weare in St Nicholas churchyard – see description opposite.

BURIAL OF MR. WEARE

It had been arranged that the body of the deceased should be interred in Elstree church-yard. Shortly before 11 o'clock, the tolling of the church bell announced that every thing was prepared for the melancholy ceremony. The coffin was borne on the shoulders of six men; the brother of the deceased and most of the Jurors attended as mourners; several persons carried lanterns before, and on either side of the coffin; and in this manner the funeral train, followed by a considerable crowd, proceeded up Elstree-hill towards the church, which is about a quarter of a mile distant from the house at which the inquest was holden. The coffin was, as in ordinary cases, first carried into the church, which was lighted up for the occasion, and then to the grave; the funeral service was read in both places by the Rev. Addow, the clergyman of the parish.As the coffin was being lowered into the grave, the rope which was placed round the foot broke, and that part of the coffin fell suddenly to the bottom of the grave, whilst the head being sustained by the other rope rested against the side of the grave, so that the coffin stood nearly upright. This unfortunate accident as might be supposed, created some confusion; but the sexton immediately descended into the grave, and by great personal exertion, in a short time succeeded in getting the coffin level at the bottom of the grave, which was about 12 feet in depth. The clergyman then proceeded to read the remainder of the funeral service and the crowd stood uncovered. The scene which now presented itself was one which can never pass from the recollection of those who witnessed it. The unusual hour of interment – the horrible and extraordinary manner in which the man whose corpse had just been consigned to the grave had lost his life – the solemn stillness of the night, for the wind which had been loud and boisterous during the day, had now fallen, and did not even shake the branches of the high trees with which the churchyard is surrounded – the impressive nature of the beautiful and affecting composition which was read by the clergyman who stood conspicuous in his white gown at the head of the grave, whilst all around him was darkness, except where the faint light of a lantern happened to fall..... The service being finished at about half-past eleven, the mourners retired from the churchyard and the grave diggers proceeded to fill up the grave.

From The Times, 2 November 1823.

---

gaiters, and a fashionable waistcoat with gilt buttons". A little before 12 noon on Friday the 9th of January 1824 Foxen pinioned Thurtell's hands in front of him with handcuffs (unusual) and he was then led from his cell to the accompaniment of the tolling prison bell and the prison chaplain reading the burial service. A few moments earlier he had confessed his guilt to the chaplain. He mounted the five steps slowly but steadily and positioned himself on the trap. Here Foxen removed his cravat and loosened his collar. When Thurtell had finished praying Foxen drew the white cotton cap over his head and placed the noose around his neck. The Governor of Hertford Gaol and the Chief Warder both shook hands with him, before Foxen adjusted the noose. Wilson said "Good bye Mr. Thurtell, may God Almighty bless you." At two minutes past midday, on the signal from Mr. Nicholson, the Under Sheriff, Foxen drew the bolts and Thurtell dropped into the trap with a crash. It was reported that his neck broke "with a sound like a pistol shot" but this is most unlikely as he would certainly not have been given sufficient length of drop for this to occur. It is probable that the reporter who made the statement got confused by the sound of the falling trap doors. However by the standards of the day Thurtell died easily and was not seen to struggle.

After hanging the customary hour his body was taken down and sent to London for dissection in Surgeons' Hall in accordance with his sentence. A waxwork of him was made and exhibited in Madame Tussauds.

114. The raised area just to the right of the footpath and behind the small gravestone is the site of Weare's unmarked grave.

Such was the excitement the killing of William Weare stimulated in 1823 that, we are told, Sir Walter Scott not only followed the murder story closely but four years after the event when returning to the north made a detour to Radlett to visit the scene of the murder, which he recorded in a diary entry for 28 May 1828,

"Our elegant researches carried us out of the high road and through a labyrinth of intricate lanes, which seem made on purpose to afford strangers the full benefit of a dark night and a drunken driver, in order to visit Gill's Hill, in Hertfordshire, famous for the murder of Mr. Weare.

The principal part of the house [Probert's cottage] is destroyed, and only the kitchen remains standing. The garden has been dismantled, though a few laurels and flowering shrubs, run wild, continue to mark the spot. The fatal pond is now only a green swamp, but so near the house that one cannot conceive how it was ever chosen as a place of temporary concealment of the murdered body." An account written around 1883 observes that maybe Scott's account is exaggerated in that "..the cottage occupied by Probert, and where Thurtell and Hunt spent the night following the murder, is still standing; it is an ordinary one-storeyed house, with a high-pitched tiled roof. In the rear is the pond which Scott describes as a 'greenswamp'.

Cussans (1881) writes that "no similar crime, probably, ever created such sensation, as did this. Books giving an account of the trial – some illustrated with steel engravings – were sold by tens of thousands. The murder was dramatized at several theatres, at one of which the yellow gig, in which the body of Weare was removed the night after the murder, and the veritable roan horse which drew it, were brought upon the stage."

FORGERY

An article in *The Times* of 23 December 1897 tells us of a charge of forgery against a Mr. William Gregory Tyler who deceived the rector of Elstree. The article is interesting if for nothing more than the names of the participants:

"The Charge of Forgery Against A Curate – William Gregory Tyler, *alias* C.W. Tyler, 29, of Williams-cottages, Boreham-wood, described on the charge-sheet as a clergyman, was again brought up in custody before Mr. Stapylton and other justices at Barnet Sessions yesterday, and charged with having obtained a situation as curate to the Rev. P.H.W. Peach, rector of Elstree, by falsely representing that he had served in service in which he had not actually served, and by means of a forged certificate of marriage was now added. Police Inspector Nutt, who searched the prisoner's lodgings, testified to finding a certificate purporting to be signed by Mr. Registrar Hazzard, and recording a marriage between William Gregory Tyler and Ada Emily Hall, solemnized at the registry office, 228 Gray's inn-road, W.C. Ada Emily Hall said she was a school teacher. She made the acquaintance of the prisoner in September, 1889, when he was editor of the *Hampshire Herald*, and they were engaged.....'

The prisoner was then committed for trial.

POLICING

Since 1805 the villages of Elstree and Boreham Wood had been patrolled by ten officers of the Bow Street Horse Patrol, stationed at Edgware. From 13 January1840, the Metropolitan Police extended their jurisdiction into Hertfordshire.

The new police were greeted with mixed feelings. The Elstree magistrates described them as being very useful, while the Rector of Elstree commented: "It appears to me very doubtful how far the contemplated constabulary force could be serviceable in this village: if there were but one constable, he would only be useful if constantly walking about in the night. By day he would be generally useless. He would probably not be sufficiently near to command the co-operation of other constables."

The force rented Elstree Cottage in the High Street from Mr Hucks Gibbs of Aldenham in 1869, although they were not happy with the rent, commenting that "the rooms are very low". In 1892 the purpose-built red brick building in Barnet Lane was opened and *Kelly's Directory* of 1894 records that the post of station sergeant was vacant and there were two acting sergeants and nine constables.

Perks, a former policemen, tells us in his *Memories of Forty Years in Elstree* that in 1927, at the end of October that "I first saw the village of Elstree, on the border of Hertfordshire and Middlesex. I was serving in the Metropolitan Police, and reported at the station in Barnet Lane, about 100 yards east of the High Street, which is part of Watling Street. This police station was built in 1892 to replace the original one, which consisted of an old cottage in the High Street near the parish church."

POLICE CUTBACKS

From July 1960 the station was closed at night leaving the public to rely on a telephone installed in a pillar in the front garden of the station, connected to a sub-divisional station. In November 1968 the station was reduced to an office and the area incorporated into Boreham Wood's section. The station closed altogether on 30 August 1971, and is now a private house.

115. The police station in Barnet Lane, built in 1892 near the junction with Elstree High Street.

116. On the face of it, rather unnecessarily, a policeman directing traffic in the 1920s at the crossroads in Elstree Village. The shops on the right were demolished to allow the widening of the junction.

POLICING IN BOREHAM WOOD

In the late 1940s the London County Council planned large estates in Boreham Wood and, with an anticipated growth in population from 9,000 in 1945 to 22,000 by 1955, the Metropolitan Police sought to open a police station there. A temporary station was built in Elstree Way, on a site purchased from the British and Dominions Film Corporation in 1955. This opened on 4 March 1957, as a sectional station of Barnet sub-division. On the same day, Shenley police station closed and all business was transferred to Boreham Wood.

The present station was built adjacent to the temporary one, and became operational on 8 July, 1968. Three years later, on 12 July 1971, the 'S' Division headquarters moved to Boreham Wood from Golders Green police station.

The responsibility for policing the new borough of Hertsmere transferred to Hertfordshire Constabulary on 1 April 2000.

Drinking Places

THE WRESTLERS AND THE BATTLE AXES

The Wrestlers stood within the now defunct hamlet of Aldenham Wood. It is probable that The Wrestlers gained its name because it was "…where at one time well-known boxers used to train, such as Nat. Langham who in 1853, beat the great Tom Sayers…" The inn was demolished in 1896 by the first Lord Aldenham, of Aldenham House when he decided to enlarge his park. This involved the destruction of Grubbs Lane, where the Wrestlers was situated and the construction of the new Grubbs Lane, soon to become Butterfly Lane, and the Battle Axes pub as a replacement. The site of the old Wrestlers is now within the Haberdashers' Aske's playing fields and recent excavations there have revealed a number of tiles and bottle fragments including a complete 19th-century bottle *(see ill. 119)*.

118. *The Gibbs coat-of-arms at the Battle Axes pub today, together with the initials of Hucks Gibbs and the date.*

117. *The Wrestlers stood near the junction of Aldenham Road and Butterfly Lane, near the Haberdashers' School playing fields.*

119. *A 19th-century bottle found during excavation of the site where the Wrestlers pub once stood.*

The Battle Axes is an unremarkable building, but reminds us of its origins in the form of a coat-of-arms containing three battleaxes, and the initials HHG, with the date 1890. These refer to Henry Hucks Gibbs, first Lord Aldenham, and the Gibbs coat of arms.

THE PLOUGH, HIGH STREET

Originally known as the Swan, the Plough has since 2003 been transformed into a Chinese restaurant, called The East, although the character of the building itself has been retained. It first appears in the records in 1637, and was held until the mid-17th century by a Samuel Feake. The Hearth Tax return of 1670 gives a Robert Montague as landlord. The present building dates to *c.* 1830. Mr Perk in his

120. *The Plough, viewed from its gardens, c.1905. The building is now The East Chinese restaurant.*

121. The Holly Bush, Elstree Hill North, one of Elstree's oldest buildings. Photo 2006.

reminiscences of Elstree tells us that in the 1920s the Plough was much favoured by actors and actresses and others from the film studios at Borehamwood. It was one of Alfred Hitchcock's favourite pubs.

THE HOLLY BUSH, HIGH STREET

The site of the Holly Bush has been occupied since at least medieval times, with the present building dating from around 1450. The first reference to it as an inn is in 1786 when it was owned by Thomas Clutterbuck, a brewer of Stanmore, Middlesex, and occupied by a John Green. Stephen Castle describes it as

"a fine example of a timber-framed hall house dating from *c*. 1450. Its two bay open hall is spanned by a massive cambered tie-beam with arch braces, above which is a cruciform-sectioned crown-post. In the surviving fragment of the original back wall is part of a window with a diamond sectioned mullion. On the north side of the hall, the flint foundations of the single bay service, demolished in the 1920s were found in 1985-1986. Adjoining the hall on the south side is a contemporary two-storeyed, two bay cross-wing, originally jettied on the High Street frontage, comprising a parlour on the ground floor and the solar or chamber on the first. A brick chimney, serving fireplaces on both floors, was inserted during the seventeenth century. At the rear of the cross-wing is a three bay timber-framed extension, including a second open hall or kitchen, apparently dating from the sixteenth century."

122. The Red Lion on the right, in Elstree High Street, c.1903. First mentioned in 1656, the building was demolished in 1936.

123. *The Artichoke public house c. 1870.*

124. *The Artichoke today.*

THE RED LION HOTEL

The Red Lion in Elstree High Street was demolished in 1936. First mentioned in 1656, kept then by Elizabeth Winterbottom, it was a stopping point for the stage coach service to London.

THE ARTICHOKE, ELSTREE HILL NORTH

The first reference is in 1750 when Philip Coghill is given as the occupier. A number of inquests took place here, notably that on William Weare (*see p89*). The inn was the stopping place of the Birmingham to London stage coach which in the 1830s called twice daily.

The building was badly damaged by fire in 1870 and the existing structure tends to hide the antiquity of the original.

125. The Farmer's Boy is second from the right. Its site is now a field.

THE FARMER'S BOY

This pub (depicted in colour on this book's jacket) stood near the corner of Elstree High Street and the Watford Road, almost at a right angle to The Plough *(qv)*. Built in the eighteenth century, its original purpose is not known, but it was probably then a private house. It became a pub around 1900. Demolition came in 1967 when the road was widened.

FISHERY INN, WATFORD ROAD

The Fishery sits alongside Aldenham reservoir and is a 1960s' structure. The original building dated from the middle of the nineteenth century.

THE CROWN, THEOBALD STREET

The history of The Crown is confusing. The original Crown stood on the north side of Theobald Street a few hundred yards north of its junction with Shenley Road. This building was mentioned in 1760 and was kept by Rebecca Gurney until 1772. At some time during the middle of the 19th century a yellow brick building was constructed in front of the original pub. To confuse matters further, in 1910 the New Crown was built on the corner of Shenley Road and Theobald Street. This building still survives as a public house and is now called The Enigma. The only part remaining of the second pub building is a stable block *(ill. 127)*. As can be seen in Illustration 126 the former Crown stood in front of a pound for stray animals.

126. The Crown, c. 1905, looking north along Theobald Street, not far from the junction with Shenley Road. Only its stable block (see ill. 127) survives. In front of the building can be seen the village pound.

127. *The former stable buildings of The Crown, which still survive in Theobald Street.*

128. *The Wellington, formerly known as the Jolly Steamer, in 2006. The existing building dates from 1908.*

THE WELLINGTON, 4 THEOBALD STREET

This pub dates from at least 1870 when it was known as the Jolly Steamer. By 1890 it assumed its current name, and was rebuilt in 1908.

The Towns Develop

GOVERNANCE

The governing body for Elstree and Boreham Wood was the Elstree parish council which came into being in 1894, holding its first meeting at the National School in Elstree on the highly unsociable 31 December of that year. Its second meeting took place a week later on 7 January 1895 when the council began to deal with the pressing matters of the day: street lighting, allotments, roads and council finances. In addition a letter was sent to Hertfordshire County Council asking for a review of the Elstree Village boundaries which were considered to be 'anomalous'. These are the very same boundaries described in *Kelly's Directory* of 1865: "[Watling Street] divides the county of Herts from Middlesex; the four parts ... are in four different parishes and two counties. The north-eastern portion, in which is the church, is in Elstree parish and Herts county; the north-western in Aldenham, Herts; the south-western in Little Stanmore, Middlesex, and the south-eastern in Edgware, Middlesex." The request was unsuccessful and the boundaries remained the same until 1 April 1993.

THE RURAL DISTRICT

Elstree Rural District, constituted in 1941, comprised three civil parishes, Elstree, which included Boreham Wood, Ridge and Shenley. The total area was just under 14 square miles. Each parish had its own parish council. The Rural District formed a part of the former Urban districts of Barnet and East Barnet, but in 1965 these latter two districts became part of the Greater London Borough of Barnet.

Elstree Rural District was then transferred to the County of Hertford, and was represented by two members on the Council. It had 19 councillors and functioned from the council offices in Shenley Road. This was a brief arrangement for in 1974 Elstree Rural District, the parish of Aldenham and the urban districts of Potters Bar and Bushey were amalgamated into the district

129. *Hertsmere Council offices in Elstree Way, Boreham Wood, in 2006.*

of Hertsmere, an artificial entity. In 1977 the district was awarded borough status by Royal Charter.

Until 1983 Hertsmere Borough Council came within the parliamentary constituency of Hertfordshire South, which was then renamed Hertsmere. The population of Hertsmere in 2004 was an estimated 93,300.

A COAT OF ARMS

A new coat of arms was devised for Hertsmere. The hart is derived from the arms of Hertfordshire County Council, although it was already a feature of the arms of Bushey UDC and Potters Bar UDC. The gateway symbolises the boundary of the

130. *The arms of Hertsmere Borough Council.*

county with Greater London, and the raised portcullis denotes the free passage between the two 'territories'. The oak is from the arms of the old Elstree RDC and represents 'Tidwulf's Tree', which also featured in the device of Watford RDC from whose area Aldenham was taken. The spool of film, of course, reflects the film industry in Elstree. The arms also include a potter's wheel from the Potters Bar UDC arms and there is also an artist's palette derived from those of Bushey UDC.[1]

FIRE FIGHTING IN ELSTREE

An attempt by Elstree Parish Council in 1907 to establish a fire fighting force was met with defeat. It was felt that the £60 cost for fire fighting equipment was excessive.

Elstree and Boreham Wood were both reliant on two small manual fire engines. One was kept at the local firm of Wellington and Ward, the other at Elstree Preparatory School in Elstree Hill South. With the formation of the Elstree Fire Brigade in 1908, both machines were put at the disposal of the force. Lack of water whilst fighting a fire in Shenley Road in 1909 led to £30 being spent on five new fire hydrants.

The captain of the fire crew was a Harry Woodgate, who was a gardener at the school. It was the development of the film industry in Boreham Wood that led to the formation of a more professional fire service. In 1931 British International Pictures instituted their own brigade which also provided a local service. Ironically, their own brigade failed to save their own studios which burned down in 1936 (*ill. 132*).

TELEPHONES

Telephones came to Elstree and Boreham Wood in 1905 and were operated by the National Telephone Company. The first subscriber was Lord Aldenham of Aldenham House, who was soon joined, after the line had been extended to Boreham Wood, by the licensee of the Crown, a dog-breeder in Theobald Street, and a surgeon in

131. Elstree Fire Brigade c.1910. The fire appliance was kept at Elstree Preparatory School.

132. *The fire brigade attached to the British International Pictures Company. They look very satisfied with themselves after fighting the 1936 fire which totally destroyed the studios. They also helped out at fires in the locality.*

Allum Lane.'[2] The Post Office took over the telephone system in 1912.

Mr Perks[3] recalls that the first telephone exchange was installed in the early part of the twentieth century in a cottage occupied by John Field and his sister Annie. When the lines increased in number it was moved to High Street House, a few feet over the border in Middlesex. The operator, however, left at 10 pm, and he didn't know what happened to calls after that time. By 1924 the telephone exchange had 97 subscribers, growing to over 500 by 1939.

THE POST OFFICE

Nineteenth and twentieth-century directories for Elstree and Boreham Wood can only make us envious of service provided by the early postal system.

Pigot's Directory for 1839 records a post office in the 'Main Street.' James Worrall was the Post Master, and that "Letters from London arrive every morning at nine and afternoon at one, and are despatched every afternoon at three and evening at seven." By 1855 Mrs Priscilla Leach Worrall was in in charge. She is still listed as being the 'receiver' in 1862, but by 1878 there was also a Post & Money Order Office & Savings Bank.

There was a pillar box listed for Boreham Wood, which was cleared at 10.40am and 6pm. By 1882 letters were delivered at 6 am, 9.30 am and 5.45pm. By 1895 in addition to the Boreham Wood pillar box, there is now one in Barnet Lane which is cleared three times daily. The transition of Boreham Wood from a rural to light industrial economy is reflected in the addition of another pillar box in Barnet Lane and by 1898 it had its own post office. Some of the increasing number of boxes were cleared up to six times every weekday.

133. *The Post Office in Elstree High Street c. 1910.*

LIBRARIES

The early Boreham Wood libraries were private, and often part of other businesses. A subscription library operated from the Boots store between Cardinal Avenue and All Saints church in Shenley Road, and, unusually, a greengrocer in Studio Parade in the 1920s ran a lending service. During the 1930s a shop called 'The Library' operated from 3 Studio Parade. The first record of a County branch library dates from the minutes of a meeting held at Boreham Wood Council School (Furzehill School) on 15 June 1936. The library was probably located at the school. In Elstree a similar scheme ran under the school mistress of the Elstree Junior Mixed School.

The development of local libraries over the next two decades reflects the growth of population. In Elstree during the 1930s the library was situated at the Chapel in Elstree. By 1939 user numbers had doubled and in 1940 a library with a stock of 2000 books opened at Glenhaven Avenue in Boreham Wood. By 1947 this had moved to Clarendon Road. Elstree meanwhile was served by a mobile library until

134. *An early improvised lending library at Anne Chessell's children's wear shop in Shenley Road.*

on 25 April 1950 it was replaced by a new library with 1000 books at Elstree Congregational Chapel. Finally a new library erected from the County Library rate was opened in Elstree Way on 6 December 1956 at a cost of £12,000. A second phase was opened in October 1963 at a cost of £17,250.[4]

GAS

Gas was originally supplied by the Elstree and Boreham Wood Gas Company formed in 1871. *Kelly's Directory* of 1890 tells us that "the place is lighted with gas from works at Boreham Wood…" Gas predominated as the main form of heating and lighting until electricity reached the area in April 1926 supplied by the North Metropolitan Power Supply Company.

WATER

Mr. Henry Robinson, who moved into Barham House on the death of the third Earl of Ranfurley, built a small water pumping station to supply the area, and residents used a small pump he installed in Theobald Street. However, with the arrival of the railway in 1868 the Colne Valley Water Company applied for parliamentary sanction to extend its services to Boreham Wood. Mr. Robinson opposed the application on the grounds that he had sunk a well there which was sufficient to supply the needs of the village. An amendment was therefore included in the Act restricting the water company to the western side of the railway. The water company started to supply water to Elstree as well from 1873, and by 1876 most dwellings had been linked with the supply.[5]

THE LOCAL PRESS

During Elstree's infancy, when Boreham Wood was little more than a hamlet attached to it, news was supplied by the *Herts Advertiser*, founded in 1855. In 1936 the area was covered by an Edgware newspaper, the *Edgware & District Post*. Reporters, such as Desmond Wilcox, a trainee at the time, were based in Burnt Oak, and would cycle over to obtain local stories. In the 1950s, the paper was bought by the *Hendon Times*, and the area was then covered by its own newspaper, the *Boreham Wood and Elstree Post* based in Shenley Road. By the 1970s this had evolved into the *Borehamwood and Elstree Times*, now based in Drayton Road, Boreham Wood, in the same building as the local museum. The paper has twice won the award for being Britain's best free newspaper. It is now part of the giant Newsquest

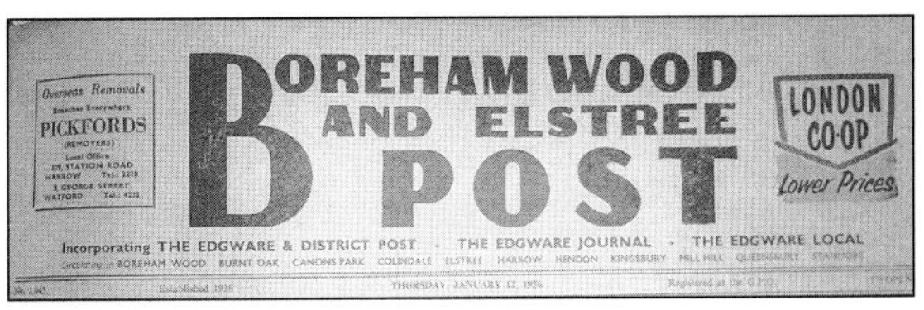

135. *The masthead of the Boreham Wood and Elstree Post in 1956.*

newspaper organisation which in itself is a subsidiary of Gannett UK Ltd.[6]

THE ELSTREE AND BOREHAM WOOD MUSEUM

The museum in Drayton Road opened in November 2000 to preserve and exhibit the history of Elstree and Boreham Wood. The displays are continually changing and the themes include the film and television industry, local personalities, and the development of the area. The collection, not all of which is on display, includes maps, photographs, items of local archaeology as well as documents. The museum is run by a number of extremely knowledgeable volunteers from the Elstree and Boreham Wood History Society, a number of whom are undertaking research into areas of specialist local history. The enthusiasm and collected knowledge of the volunteers makes this museum well worth a visit. The venture is supported by Hertsmere Borough Council as well as a number of local businesses.

1   Courtesy of Civic Heraldy of England and Wales
2   Frewin p 39
3   W H Perks in 'My memories of forty years in Elstree' in *Hertfordshire Countryside*, Aug. 1971, pp 50-51
4   I am indebted to Lesley Davies of the Elstree & Boreham Wood Museum for providing me with the results of her extensive research into the history of libraries in Boreham Wood.
5   Frewin, p38
6   I am grateful to Rod Brewster, former editor of the *Borehamwood and Elstree Times* for much information.

The British Hollywood

Elstree, in terms of the film industry, is actually Boreham Wood. It is known as the 'British Hollywood' for the simple reason that outside of Hollywood it is the single most concentrated centre of film and television studios anywhere in the western world. Once there were seven studios, today there are four. As Joe Utichi and Scott Andrews say in their internet article[1], "During the studios' heyday the people and pubs of the town became accustomed to seeing Tony Hancock and Yul Brynner sharing a pint, or Indiana Jones strolling along the road to the newsagents. A strange mixture of high glamour and fish and chip shop small town England, Elstree holds a unique place in the history of world cinema."

NEPTUNE AND AFTER

The BBC's Elstree Centre is Elstree's oldest film studio, opening in 1914 in Clarendon Road as Neptune Studios, "lured there by the fog-free air (at this time the capital still suffered choking smogs on a regular basis, hardly ideal for filming!), lush scenery for location work, and easy transport links into town. From the very beginning Elstree was the scene of innovation and experimentation – Neptune's sound stage was entirely devoid of windows, making it the very first 'dark stage' outside the United States.'[2]

136. This Ordnance Survey map of 1935 shows the layout and location of the studios along Shenley Road and Elstree Way.

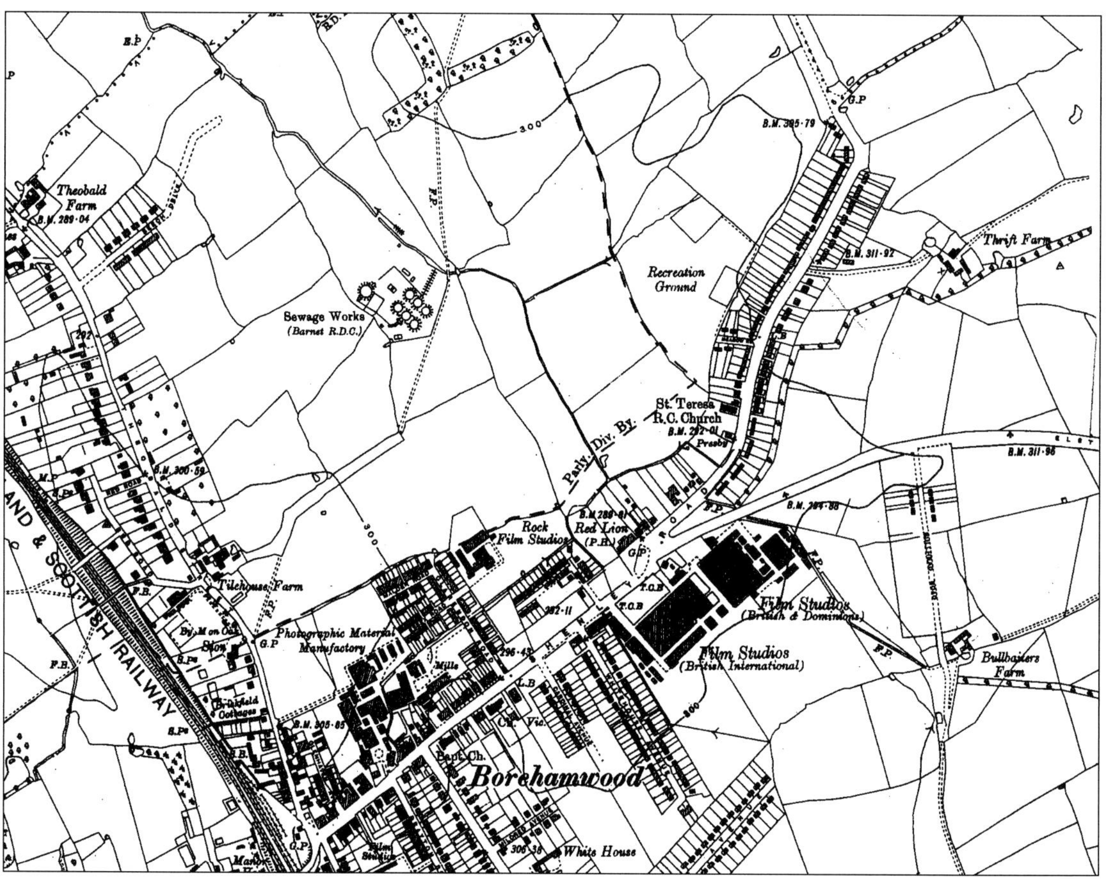

137. *The Gate Studios in February 2006 shortly before the final stage of demolition. A valuable part of Elstree's film heritage is now lost. Note the 'crow's nest' peeking up above the skyline where lookouts watched for trains in order to warn the production units of their impending noise.*

Between 1914 and the 1950s, under different owners, Neptune produced a large number of low budget British movies. Well-known names of the time that worked here include Deborah Kerr, Stewart Granger, and George Formby. During the 1950s the emphasis moved to television production. It was here that programmes such as *William Tell* and *The Invisible Man* were produced. In 1960 Lew Grade's ATV purchased the studio. With him at the helm productions such as *Family Fortunes*, *The Muppet Show* and *Aufwiedersehen Pet* made their way to our television screens. In 1983 the BBC, which needed somewhere with a small backlot, bought it to run a new soap, *EastEnders*. This commenced in 1985 and continues to be produced there, though there are occasional rumours as to the future of the series.

THE MGM STUDIOS

MGM was one of the largest studios in Europe, covering an area of 120 acres between the present Studio Way and Potters and Rowley Lanes opposite the Elstree Studios – its site is now covered by a housing estate. It was built prior to the Second World War and was operated by Metro Goldwyn Mayer from 1944 to 1970 when the facility was closed. Some of the better known films produced here were *Ivanhoe* with Robert Taylor, and Stanley Kubrick's *2001: A Space Odyssey*. Paul Welsh, the historian of the British Hollywood, says that "MGM was probably the most glamorous of studios we had in the town…if you think of Elstree [Studios] today, which is fifteen acres, [MGM] was 115 acres and had a beautiful back-lot which is now all housing. They built the castle for the *Ivanhoe* film there which stood for about six years on the landscape, so people thought it was a real castle. It was built to last, and it did.

THE GATE STUDIOS

During the silent era Whitehall Studios produced films in Station Road directly opposite Elstree & Boreham Wood station. There was no particular difficulty then in setting up a production unit directly opposite a busy and noisy railway station, "...but, with the change to talkies, Whitehall found themselves with a problem. Situated next to a railway line, the sound stages rattled and echoed with the regular passing of the London express. A crow's nest was built and fitted with a buzzer and a luckless runner would sit on his perch all day with a pair of binoculars, scanning the horizon for telltale puffs of steam. When the train was on its way he would buzz the soundstage and filming would pause as the engine thundered past!"

The Gate Studios were built in 1928, on the site of Whitehall Studios in Station Road, opposite the station. They specialised in religious themed movies because the chairman of the Rank Organisation, J. Arthur Rank, was a devout Methodist. Most of the productions were fairly low-key British films – the best known being *Odette*, which starred Anna Neagle and Trevor Howard. Harkness Screens, manufacturer of cinema screens, took over the unit in the mid 1950s, shipping their products to cinemas all over the world. Harkness moved out in 2003 and despite much local opposition, the unit was demolished in February 2006 to make way for a housing development.

THE FAST FOOD OF FILMING

The only Elstree studio to have been situated in Elstree itself belonged to the 'legendary' Danziger brothers. It was situated near the Fishery Inn on the Watford Road opposite the Aldenham Reservoir. The site now lies under an office and industrial estate, although there is a plaque *(ill. 138)* on the gates commemorating the studio's presence between 1956 and 1961.

The company specialised in turning out high volume, low quality 'B' movies with a shooting schedule that typically lasted no more than five days from beginning to end. Tv programmes were allocated two days and second and third

138. *A plaque next to the gates of the Waterfront Industrial Estate commemorates Danzigers – the only film studio that was situated in Elstree itself.*

takes were not allowed. If a film appeared to be running behind schedule, Danziger would rip some pages out of the script and inform the producer that he was now back on schedule. The Danzigers sold the studios in 1965 for £300,000.

ELSTREE STUDIOS

Elstree Studios opened in the 1920s in Shenley Road. The 1950s saw the filming here of a number of classic films. These included *The Dam Busters*, *Moby Dick* and *Look Back in Anger*. It is an interesting thought that some of cinema's most famous stars could be seen in the streets of Elstree and Boreham Wood. Among the most prominent were Gregory Peck, Ronald Reagan, David Niven, Audrey Hepburn, Errol Flynn and Richard Attenborough.

The studios successfully adapted to the changing trends of the 1960s. The growth of television was at first seen as a threat to the cinema, but the studios expanded into television production. Some of the better known results of this are *The Avengers* and *The Saint*. Success in film making was highlighted in 1977 with the phenomenal, but unexpected success of George Lucas's space adventure, *Star Wars* which starred Alec Guinness. The studios rented out the stages at a flat fee or were offered the option of a percentage of the profits. The studio's decision to turn down this offer – on what was seen as a risky gamble – was to cost them dear. Alec Guinness, on the other hand, made a fortune from having a percentage interest in a role which he despised.

Lucas was involved in the writing of a number of further successes which kept Elstree Studios to the fore. In 1978, Stanley Kubrick brought his adaptation of Stephen King's *The Shining* to the studios. Further notable films were *The Empire Strikes Back*, released in 1980, *Raiders of the Lost Ark* (1981) and *The Return of the Jedi* (1983). Again, the studio declined an interest in *Raiders* and lost out once more.

The 1980s almost saw the total demise of the studios, now owned by Cannon, an American company. A downturn in production led to Cannon selling the studios and the large plot of land that went with them to the Brent Walker Entertainment Group. In 1988 Brent Walker attempted to revive the studios by production there for Goldcrest Studios, another company they owned.

This venture failed and with the banks now overseeing matters, twelve acres of the site were sold off in 1990 and the Tesco supermarket was built. The area where *Star Wars* was filmed is now displaced by the frozen food aisle.

The studios closed from 1993 and 1996 and Brent Walker proposed to sell the rest of the site for development. Hertsmere Council put a stop to that and threatened a compulsory purchase of what was left of the studios. In the event the council did buy the property and in 1999 production resumed with the building of two new stages.

The studios are now known as the Elstree Film and Television Studios and have returned to national prominence in that they play host to television's *Who Wants to be a Millionaire?* and *Big Brother*.

An important figure in the saving of Elstree Studios and indeed much of Elstree's film heritage has been Paul Welsh, the council's Entertainments Officer and the local film historian.

Joe Utichi and Scott Andrews, media

139. Elstree Film Studios in 2006. Much more now lies underneath the Tesco Superstore, including the location where Star Wars *was filmed.*

140.   *The visit of King George V and Queen Mary to British International Pictures on 31 May 1934.*

journalists, summarise Welsh, and the Elstree film ethos succinctly:

"He's a man who's been immersed in the town's filmic roots since he was a boy collecting autographs from the greatest actors ever to hit the big screen but his understanding of the history of film in Elstree and Borehamwood goes much deeper than his experience."[1]

Welsh describes the town as having a chequered past when it comes to film production. With the highs, come the lows. "I've seen things thrown into skips that you could cry about," he says, of the loss of part of the studios to Tesco, "I've seen scripts discarded, props from *Star Wars* that would cost a fortune now to buy abandoned, documents from Hitchcock's *Blackmail* dumped into a skip. In the late sixties they had a library of screen tests that they'd done on actors - Richard Harris, Audrey Hepburn, Laurence Olivier, a whole cast of people who'd gone through the studio, and an executive of the time just stopped by and said, 'what's the purpose of keeping the junk?' and they just scrapped it all."

Welsh has made some observations which sum up the sometimes unreal and, on the face of it, very ordinary nature of Britain's Hollywood. Well-known faces integrate seamlessly with the local residents, and have always done so. The McDonalds situated almost opposite the studios was until recent years The Red Lion which in times past was frequented by the likes of Tony Hancock and Errol Flynn. It was typical of the town's logic that no one used to bat an eyelid. "People didn't notice it", Welsh continues. "Because the town is built around people working in the industry, it didn't mean a great deal. I walked down to the village once to the bookshop with Anthony Quinn, who was doing *The Greek Tycoon* at Elstree, because he needed a copy of his autobiography to give to a journalist who was doing an interview with him."

141. Uniformed staff of British International Pictures in the 1930s.

BRITISH AND DOMINIONS IMPERIAL STUDIOS

These studios opened in 1925 as British National Pictures. In 1927 they were taken over by British International Pictures. They were the first purpose-built sound studios in Europe, and here the first ever British sound movie was made here in 1929 called *Blackmail*, directed by Alfred Hitchcock. Among the stars who worked here were Leslie Howard and Anna Neagle and it was also here that Douglas Fairbanks senior made his final screen appearance. The life of the studios was short, being destroyed by fire on 9 February 1936.

HOMES TO THE STARS

Richard Tauber, (1891-1948) described as the greatest Mozart tenor of his time lived at Villa Capri in Allum Lane. It was a white villa-style house with shutters, surrounded by foliage. Fred Emney (1900-1980), a prolific actor, lived in Barham Avenue. Dana Wynter of *Sink the Bismarck* and *Invasion of the Bodysnatchers* lived in Clarendon Road, Boreham Wood. In the 1950s and '60s Abbots Mead in Barnet Lane was the home of the Cowell family of Simon Cowell fame. They sold the house to film director Stanley Kubrick who lived there until the 1980s. Friars Mead, another house in Barnet Lane was purchased in the 1963 by Joan Collins and Anthony Newley, but they never lived there. The Chantry in Barnet Lane was used on a rental basis by the film studios to house their transitory stars. One of the more dramatic events by which this house is remembered was the theft of Sophia Loren's jewelry whilst staying there in the 1960s. At the time she was making *The Millionairess* at the nearby MGM Studios. A burglar confessed to the robbery in the 1990s.

Dame Anna Neagle (1904-1986) lived in a house on the corner of Deacon's Hill Road and Barnet Lane called Hartfield. This has since been demolished but the name lives on in the form of Hartfield Avenue.

THE ELSTREE FILM & TELEVISION HERITAGE GROUP

One of the most important parts of the district's cultural heritage is its links with the film and television industry. It is not unusual that if one lives or works within a town which wears its heritage with a comfortable ease, that one tends to either ignore or disregard it. This is very much the situation in Boreham Wood which has lately allowed a major part of its film heritage, the Gate Studios, the UK's oldest remaining sound stage to go to its destruction. It is to preserve and record an important heritage that the Elstree Film & Television Heritage Group was established by a group of local volunteers in May 2005. The group has recorded the memories of a number of people who worked at the studios as well as collected images of the building's last days. The group chairman is Paul Welsh, who writes a weekly column on the subject for the *Borehamwood and Elstree Times*. The Group has a number of plans which include public displays, projects with students and staff at Hertswood the specialist arts college, screenings of local film classics and an exhibition to celebrate almost 25 years at Boreham Wood.

142. Imperial Place now stands on the site of British International Pictures.

Support has come from companies like Elstree Film and Television Studios and large organisations like the Broadcasting Entertainment Cinematograph, the Theatre Union, the British Film Institute and the Museum of London.

[1] I am grateful to Elstree Film Studios, Joe Utichi & Scott Andrews for allowing me to use their article in this section. http://www.elstreefilmtv.com/

Leisure Times

ALDENHAM RESERVOIR

Aldenham Reservoir was constructed by the Grand Junction Canal Company after the passing of an Act of Parliament dated 1793. It was formed on what had been a part of Aldenham Common with the purpose of "… collecting flood waters to supply the River Gade, and Colne, for the benefit of the mills thereon, with a quantity of water equal to that taken therefrom for the use of the canal." From this time on it provided the local inhabitants with a number of sporting pastimes, as it still does.

The reservoir, originally called Elstree Reservoir, became a popular local feature from its earliest days. William Charles Macready (1793-1873) one of the best-known actors of the nineteenth century, and a close friend of Charles Dickens, leased Elm Place nearby in 1831 for nine years. His diaries tell us that he loved to walk in the vicinity and row on the reservoir and that when his son Henry was christened at Elstree in August 1839, after the ceremony, Macready and Charles Dickens rowed on the reservoir. *Pigot's Directory* of 1839 comments that "the reservoir … forms a delightful lake embellishment to the village." *Kelly's Directory* of 1878 notes that "To the west of the village is situated a reservoir of 200 acres, which affords excellent boating and fishing, and is much frequented", and Walford in his 1883 *Greater London* says of the reservoir that "..it has become a favourite haunt for wild fowl and waders." He continues, "... the reservoir is well known to London ornithologists and anglers. It is a beautiful lake, nearly one hundred acres in extent, embosomed in grassy hills, secluded with aquatic trees, and consequently the great attraction of the place."

The reservoir had its dark side. There are a number of entries in the St Nicholas parish

143. *The view across Aldenham Reservoir towards Elstree Village, May 1822 (see also illustration 145).*

register for the nineteenth century that shows that children during this period lost their lives by drowning whilst swimming there. A sad double tragedy is recorded in *The Times* of 6 June 1891:

Yesterday the Herts Coroner held an inquiry at the Fishery Inn, Elstree, into the circumstances attending the death by drowning in Elstree reservoir of PETER VANDENHEUVEL and LAMBERT WERNER, both aged 22, Dutch students at the Roman Catholic Theological College at Mill Hill. A student at the college named Vandenbesien stated that on Thursday evening he went with four other students, including the deceased to bathe in Elstree reservoir. When some distance from the shore with two of his companions he noticed Vandenheuvel and Werner splashing near the shore and remarked that they seemed to be in trouble. His companions replied that they were only playing, but they subsequently disappeared, and when the witness swam to the spot, although he dived several times, he could not discover them. Neither of the deceased gentlemen could swim. Abraham Ellwood, a labourer, said that he was watching the bathers. The one of the two who was nearest to the shore got into trouble and sank. His comrade went to his assistance and caught him as he rose. The drowning man threw his arms around his rescuer and in the struggle both went under and disappeared.

145. *Aldenham Reservoir 2006 – the same view as illustration 143.*

MEN AND MAIDENS

Harold Knee recalls that about the year 1912 he was a member of Radlett Rowing Club:

"We practised our rowing on the reservoir at Elstree ... and for quite a number of years it was possible to hire rowing boats, skiffs and punts; one has always been able to fish there. Weekends brought many young men and maidens, mums and dads and their families to the reservoir for the boating and one could get a good tea there as well. Years later, they even brought loads of

144. *Aldenham Reservoir c. 1905.*

146. One of the many facilities offered in the Aldenham Country Park is the above, together with fishing, sailing, playgrounds and on some Saturdays, a farmers' market.

147. Boreham Rovers, 1932-3, forerunners of Boreham Wood Football Club.

good sand to the 'Rezzy', as we called it, and made a Lido which was very well patronised, but with the advent of the Second World War boating and teas came to an end, as did the Lido as well …"

BOREHAM WOOD FOOTBALL CLUB

Bill O'Neill in his exhaustive history of Boreham Wood Football Club believes that it was originally formed in the 1890s as 'Tunnel United'. This unusual name was attributed to the team comprised of workers building the railway tunnel from Elstree to Mill Hill. O'Neill says that when the tunnel was completed the locals took it over. Boreham Wood Football Club does not officially enter the scene until 1935.[1]

A CONVENIENT CINEMA – THE GEM

No. 1 Station Road, opposite the booking hall of Elstree station, was until recently a public lavatory and is now a flower shop. The building

148. A former Baptist chapel, which in 1914 became the Gem Cinema. It is now a flower shop.

has experienced a diverse past. It began as a Baptist chapel in 1894, and when the Baptists moved out in 1911 to Shenley Road, the building was taken over by the Neptune Film Company as a film studio *(see p106).* "Reputedly seating a maximum of 150 squeezed onto wooden benches, it may have served as a private viewing theatre for the company, as well as a public cinema in the evenings, showing Neptune's productions and others. Charging admission prices of 1d, 2d and 3d, it apparently claimed to be the smallest cinema in the world. The Neptune Company ceased productions and the studio passed to new owners in 1917. Whether the cinema closed at this time has not been established."[2]

At some stage the building was used in an administrative role by the local council, before being converted into a public convenience. An early memory from a 1981 *Boreham Wood Post* gives us the flavour of an evening there:

> "I reflected with nostalgia that, where trap No.2 in the gents' now stands, was the exact spot upon which stood the honky-tonk piano. I could once more hear the pianist hammering out the old and familiar diddle-diddle-dum ... Owing to the bad quality of the film in those days and the constant friction of bad projection, every

episode appeared to be enacted in a torrential rainstorm ... in seeking such entertainment we suffered many hazards. I cannot remember a single performance being given without something going wrong ... there was no electricity and the projector was illuminated by what was called a limelight ... the bottle of hydrogen gas ran out, usually halfway through the performance. There would then be a delay of some twenty minutes, while the proprietor and the projectionist made a frenzied dash over the fence to the railway station to see if a new bottle of gas had arrived by a late passenger train. If it had, all well and good. But if it had not, we the audience were invited by the panting proprietor to receive our money back at the paybox on our way out."

The building stood empty between 1996 and 1998, before becoming the Eau de Toilette flower shop. The shop entrance to what is now Paradise Flowers was previously the entrance to the Ladies.

STUDIO/STUDIO 70 AT 231 SHENLEY ROAD

In February 1935 Tudor Cinemas of Elstree submitted plans for a 'Tudor Style' cinema with 'an olde English' garden and a baronial style hall for the foyer – even the staff would be dressed in Tudor costume. Barnet Rural Council rejected the scheme as too large for the area. The building that followed seated 820 persons. Situated firmly in Boreham Wood it advertised itself as the 'Studio Elstree'. The cinema was particularly successful during the 1940s and 1950s. The area under the stage contained a giant popcorn machine which had come from America for Douglas Fairbanks Jnr who had been filming in Elstree, and was subsequently given to the cinema. The cinema was closed for 3 months for alterations in 1966, re-opening with the then futuristic name of 'Studio 70.' The first film to be shown on its re-opening was *Carry on Cowboy.* However, the cinema began to fail and was put up for sale. Its final double-bill showing of *Stir Crazy* and *California Suite* took place on Saturday, 6 June 1981. The building was demolished in

149. The Venue Leisure Centre, opened in October 2000 at a cost of £18 million. Photo 2006.

December 1981:

"...its large illuminated signboard was bought for the Civic Hall on Elstree Way where films were already being regularly shown in the 662-seat auditorium. (This later became the Hertsmere Centre and The Venue before being demolished in October 1997 for a new theatre that was never built.) The Studio cinema's site is occupied by part of two office blocks..."[4]

THE CINEMA/OMNIPLEX (NOW THE POINT), 84 SHENLEY ROAD

The cinema opened in January 1999 with four auditoria. Ironically, in a town so closely associated with film production and television, it had poor audience figures and closed in September 2000. In 2002 the cinema reopened as The Point.

THE VENUE

Boreham Wood and Elstree are well served by a number of health complexes. The largest and most prominent is the Hertsmere funded Venue in Elstree Way, Boreham Wood. This is a well-equipped leisure facility which cost £18 million pounds to build and opened in October 2000. It attracts in the region of 500,000 visitors per year and features, in addition to a full health club, a 25-metre eight-lane swimming pool. Nearby is the Hertswood Centre, formerly known as the Hawksmoor Centre, which was reopened in June 1997 following a £1.5 million refurbishment.

1   Bill O'Neill, The Story of Boreham Wood Football Club 1935-2005

2   Eyles and Skone, Cinemas of Hertfordshire, pp33-4

3   *Ibid*

4   *Ibid* p37

Elstree Aerodrome

Elstree Aerodrome, (originally known as Aldenham Aerodrome), was founded in 1934, as an adjunct to Aldenham House which, after the death of the then owner Vicary Gibbs in 1932, was leased to a Captain (later Brigadier) William Watkins who converted the now empty house into a country club and residential health resort known as the Aldenham House Club. This needed a landing area for visiting members. There was probably an unofficial landing ground on the Aldenham Estate as early as 1930. "Facilities were minimal, consisting only of a petrol pump and a wooden hut containing a telephone." [1]

A licence was officially granted in April 1934.

"An inspection by the Air Ministry on 19 September noted that the wooden frame of a hangar was under construction but that there were no other buildings on the site ... the Inspector considered that the proximity of high tension cables and their attendant pylons rendered the site unsafe for flying instruction and therefore unsuitable for licensing as a permanent aerodrome. These cables were to prove a major obstacle to any expansion of the aerodrome in the future." [2]

This however did not stop a number of aviation companies taking up residence and despite the Inspector's reservations, they did not stop flying training taking place there, which commenced in 1935 under the auspices of the London Air Park Flying Club. The club, popular with Hollywood film producers taking flying lessons, was finally shut down by the Air Ministry in late 1937.

Aldenham Aerodrome was officially opened on 20 April 1935. The then grass landing strip was 750 yards. The aerodrome continued to maintain an elite image: "A regular visitor to Aldenham in the mid-1930s was the Duchess of Bedford, who would park her aeroplane at the aerodrome and travel into London by car. Her log books reveal that she made fourteen flights into Aldenham between June 1935 and July 1936,

often accompanied by her personal pilot Flt Lt Rupert C.Preston ... The 72-year-old Duchess took off from her airstrip on the Woburn estate on 22 March 1937 to try to complete 200 flying hours and was never seen again." [3]

By 1937 Aldenham Aerodrome was being referred to as Elstree Aerodrome in aviation literature. By 1939 the poor surface and the high tension cables led to its licence being suspended. A pilot's log book from the period just prior to the suspension reads: "frightening take-off due to rough ground", "slow take-off due to mud", "almost under water, boggy in places." [4]

The advent of war brought the aerodrome back into use. During this period the aerodrome was taken over by the Ministry of Aircraft Production, which built three new hangars and a concrete runway for the repair of Wellington bombers. The site was also used for ferrying secret agents to and from occupied Europe. It was during this period that the grass runway was concreted.

After the war, there was a brief surge in private aviation, but by 1950 most of the resident companies had moved away and the wartime hangars had deteriorated considerably. The site's managers, London Aero & Motor Services (LAMS) used the airfield to fly in converted Halifax bombers loaded with food from Italy due to the food shortages at the time. But when one of the bombers went through the runway, tearing off the undercarriage and ending up on its belly some distance from its intended rest point, LAMS decided to relocate to Stansted Airport. The firm's Elstree staff were given their notices and the aerodrome was in danger of closing down.

The aerodrome has withstood these misfortunes and is now a busy airfield for light aircraft undoubtedly due to its proximity to London and the suburbs. Flying training and charters still operate after 70 years.

1   Riding and Peerless, *Elstree aerodrome: the past in pictures*, pp 12-13
2   *Ibid* p13
3   *Ibid* p17
4   *Ibid* p18

Wartimes

FIRST WORLD WAR

The Elstree and Boreham Wood Museum is the home of memories and artefacts relating to both World Wars. The number of local memorials indicate the vast number of lives lost in this war, to the extent that it decimated the tiniest of villages. The Elstree Village memorial was dedicated on 14 July 1921 and the Boreham Wood Memorial in Theobald Street on 20 October – shortly afterwards it was moved to the end of Shenley Road near the Hertsmere civic offices. Letchmore Heath, Radlett and Aldenham, have their own memorials. Plaques on cottage walls and in local churches and schools are also reminders of those who went off to war in the years after 1914 and never returned.

There are also a number of houses in the area which have plaques.

One soldier who did not return was William, the eldest son of Edward and Charlotte Mason of High Street, Elstree, who had left for Canada in November 1913:

"As soon as war was declared in August 1914, William's brother Alfred enlisted with the 9th Middlesex and in 1915 another brother, Montague, joined the Hertfordshire Royal Horse Artillery as a driver. The following month their father, Edward Mason 45, also enlisted as a driver but was later discharged as physically unfit. Meanwhile, regiments were being formed in Canada and in the April of 1916 William Mason enlisted with the Canadian Expeditionary Force. He returned to England the following month and by June was in France with the 58th Bn Canadian infantry Central Ontario Regiment, shortly before the commencement of the Battle of the Somme on 1st July 1916. William Mason was reported missing, presumed killed, on 20th September 1916. He was subsequently buried in Courcelette Cemetery, also the resting place of a

150. An early photograph of the Elstree Village war memorial, dedicated on 14 July 1921.

151. The Boreham Wood war memorial, dedicated on 20 October 1921, in its original position in Theobald Street.

152. Close up of the Boreham Wood war memorial in its present position in Shenley Road.

153. The All Saints churchyard grave of Corporal B Binoth of the Royal Air Force who died in March 1942 at the age of 26.

neighbouring Boreham Wood man named Eustace T. Stow."[1]

The number of Boreham Wood men who joined up was 276, the number who died was 39, giving a percentage death rate of 14% against the national average of 11%.

THE SECOND WORLD WAR

Elstree, Boreham Wood, Radlett and the surrounding area played a key role in the defence of the British Isles in the Second World War. Peter Johnson wrote in his *Elstree Childhood* that "...the R.A.F. had a headquarters in Stanmore, bombers were manufactured at Park Street and Hatfield and many factories in Boreham Wood supplied parts. Goering's bombers were thwarted by our *'beam-benders'* operating in Radlett. The S.O.E. ran secret operations from the *Thatched Barn* on the A1. [The Elstree Moat House now stands on the site.] Elstree Studios assembled a massive 10-division dummy army that deceived the Germans on D-Day, shortened the war and saved many lives."[2]

Elstree Aerodrome, the airfield at Radlett, as well as Aldenham House all played important roles. There was a Polish army camp in Theobald Street in the vicinity of Chatsworth Close. A German P.O.W. camp was located in Station Road near the gasworks, and Ripon Close housed an Italian camp, and of this camp Peter Johnson:

"We had an Italian prisoner of war camp near Elstree at the top of Allum Lane, and they could have been living at Radnor Hall close to Mr Munt's stables. They seemed to have a lot of freedom and appeared happy with their lot. During the day they went out to work on farms, and in the evening they would queue up outside the cinema with the rest of us. They all wore a greenish hat and a very long dark overcoat with a green circular patch sown onto the back for easy identification. At first we didn't like them, they were the enemy, but after a time grudgingly accepted them."

Johnson continues:

"...nearly all the large houses in the village, mainly in Barnet Lane, were requisitioned by the army for the duration of the war, including the preparatory school on Elstree Hill South which had relocated to Woolhampton Park,

154. The Elstree regiment of the Home Guard in training during the Second World War.

155. The Boreham Wood regiment of the Home Guard.

Berkshire in September 1939. Playing fields became assault courses, landscaped gardens became rifle ranges, and any gardens with water features, such as the pond on the left hand side of the driveway into Abbotsbury were used to practise building Bailey bridges, a simple but effective temporary military bridge."[3]

DESTRUCTION

Both Elstree and Boreham Wood were struck on a number of occasions – though injuries were few. On 5 January 1940 a high explosive bomb fell in the dip in Allum Lane next to Nicoll Farm. In nearby Letchmore Heath on the night of the 25 September 1940 a bomb 'ditched' by a German pilot struck the Bricklayers Arms public house which stood on the corner of Common Lane and Back Lane, killing the landlady and a little girl who had been sheltering in the cellar, and on 27 September 1940 a bomb fell on The Fortune, a house in Barnet Lane, killing four of the five occupants. The same bomb did some damage to Elstree School.

On 14 October 1940 a bomb fell on 299 Shenley Road – Kathy Gates describes what happened – "our family was in bed when the bomb fell. I was injured when my wardrobe fell and trapped me. Luckily the rest of my family were unharmed.

Having been rescued, an army vehicle gave me a bumpy ride to Barnet Hospital, which was crammed with casualties who mainly came from the East End..." A house on the corner of Cardinal Avenue and Hillside Avenue was destroyed by a high explosive bomb in November 1940. A V1 (flying bomb known as a doodlebug) fell in a field 50 yards from Tennison Avenue during the early hours of 23 June 1944.

Beryl Smith recalls "On the night of the bombing, the air raid warning sounded and as was normal our family made their way to the Anderson shelter in the garden. The raid had been on for a while, when my father decided to go back into the house to listen to the nine o'clock news. He had only been in the house for a short while when the bomb dropped. I remember being lifted off my bunk by the blast and falling back onto it. In the shelter we were all in a state of shock and were worried about what had happened to my father. Fortunately none of us in the shelter was injured. I was only seven years old at the time, and after debris had been cleared from the shelter entrance, my mother wrapped me in a blanket, and carried me to the bottom of the garden where the Ray family lived."[4]

Like the Smiths, the Rays were taking cover in

156. Shelter practice at the Keystone works, Boreham Wood.

their Anderson shelter when the bomb dropped. George Ray, who was fourteen at the time, remembers the bomb falling.

"After the bomb dropped, we waited a while and then my mother got up and told me to stay in the shelter while she went to see what had happened. Being an inquisitive lad, I followed her to the bottom of the garden where I was able to see the extent of the damage, and help her lift Beryl over the fence. Beryl's father, Bert, was dug out of the debris forty minutes after the bomb dropped. When the bomb exploded he had been thrown across the room and had hit the family piano. He was also injured by falling debris and suffered a broken jaw and broken leg in addition to having a nail pierce his jaw. He was taken to Barnet Hospital, where the following day, he was joined by another local casualty."

DAD'S ARMY

The Home Guard was a voluntary force set up in May 1940, when the German forces were sweeping through Europe and the likelihood of an invasion of the British Isles seemed very real.

Due to the slightly older nature of its volunteers, who ranged between 17 and 65, the Home Guard soon became known as 'Dad's Army.' Within the boundaries of the Elstree Rural District, three units were formed, Elstree, Boreham Wood and Shenley. They were part of the 19th Battalion of the Middlesex Regiment. Their headquarters was Elm Lodge. Some memories of the period come from Jim Read who joined the Home Guard as a runner at the age of 15 in 1941:

"One very dark night, we went out on a march on the path around Elstree Reservoir. We were marching in twos, and I was with 'Dobber' Smith (a WW1 veteran who had taken me under his wing). Suddenly Dobber told me to stop, and the rest of the platoon marched on – into the reservoir!"

1   Courtesy Elstree and Boreham Wood Museum
2   Peter Johnson, *My Elstree Childhood*, p9
3   *Ibid*
4   Courtesy Elstree and Boreham Wood Museum

Appendices

PLACE NAMES
Early versions of the place names Elstree and Boreham Wood are as follows:
Tidulfes treow 785
Tidilvestre 1188
Tydolvestre 1214-35
Idulfestre c. 1275
Idolvestre 1254
Ydolvestre 1278
Idelestre 1320
Idelstre 1331
Illestre 1487, 1502, 1550
Illestree 1536
Elstre 1698
Ilstrey 1610
Elstree, Idelstrey, Elstrey 1675
Elstre or Eaglestrey 1750

Bosci de Borham 1188
Boreham 1301
wood of Boreham 1203
Borham 1272, 1281
Burhamwode 13th century
Borhamwode 1329
Barramwoode 1554

GEOLOGY
Elstree, located on the borders of Hertfordshire and the former Middlesex, sits on the crest of a conspicuous but broken ridge which runs from Batchworth Heath, near Harefield, via Oxhey to Elstree and thence eastward to within two miles of Barnet. Elstree is unusual in that it lies within a number of geographical boundaries. The highest points in the county lie along its northern border: Oxhey Hill (438ft), Harrow Weald Common (475ft), Bushey Heath (504ft), Deacon's Hill, Edgware (478ft) and Highwood Hill (443ft).

The upper part of the London Clay is appreciably sandy or loamy. This, the 'upper sandy London Clay' of certain older writers, is now distinguished as the Claygate Beds, which form part of the upper slopes of the hills at Harrow, Hampstead and Highgate. These beds provide a natural brickmaking mixture and yield soil lighter than that of the main mass of the London Clay, more readily amenable to arable cultivation. This explains the number of early kilns and brickworks in the Elstree and Radlett areas.

Pebble Gravel, 6-10ft or less in thickness, caps the highest summits in isolated patches which are evidently the remnants of a once wide-spreading formation. It is composed of rounded flint pebbles, derived from the Eocene deposits, mixed with other far-travelled constituents, notably small, white quartz pebbles. This deposit may be either an old sea floor, or a gravel-strewn river plain, but it marks the initial surface on which the present streams began their life. The age of the Pebble Gravel may be as early Pleistocene and the whole of the London valley has been formed since that time. This occurrence of Pebble Gravels includes Brockley Hill, Elstree and Woodcock Hill.

THE DOMESDAY SURVEY 1086
The Domesday Book entry for the area is as follows:
'In Titeberst, Adam holds half a hide of the Bishop of Bayeux. Arable is two bovates. There is one bordar. Pannage for twenty hogs. It is worth ten shillings; when received five shillings, and the same in the time of King Edward. Alward held this land of the Abbot of St Albans, and could not sell it without his licence.

The Abbot of Westminster holds one hide in Titeberst. Arable is half a carucate. Pannage for forty hogs. It is and was worth ten shilings; in the time of King Edward thirteen shillings and fourpence.

Geoffrey de Mandeville holds in the same vill three virgates of the Abbot of Westminster. Arable is half a carucate. Pannage for twelve hogs. It is and was worth six shillings and eightpence: in the time of King Edward ten shillings.

Geoffrey de Bech holds half a hide in Titeberst of the Abbot of St Albans. It is and always was worth six shillings. A certain socman, a thane of the Abbot of St Albans, held it in the time of King Edward. He had no power to sell it from the church.

Geoffrey de Mandeville holds in Titeberst, and Ralph of him, three virgates. Arable is half a carucate. There is one villein with one bordar. Pannage for twelve hogs. It is and was worth five shillings: in the time of King Edward ten shillings. Three socmen held this land, two of them were thanes of Augar, Master of the Horse; the third was a thane of St Albans. He could not sell it, but the other two could.

In Titeberst, Louet holds of Geoffrey de Bech half a hide. Arable is six bovates. There is one villein. Pannage for twenty-four hogs. It is and always was worth five shillings. A socman of the Abbot of St Albans held this land, and could sell it.

Bibliography

Avery, J R: *The Story of Aldenham House* (from the archivist at Haberdashers' Aske's School).

Brooks, W C: 'Barham House', *Hertfordshire Countryside*, Nov. 1968, pp 20-21.

Castle, Stephen A: *Excavations at Brockley Hill, Middlesex Sulloniacae, 1970 (1972).*

Castle: *Elstree & Boreham Wood in camera: a nostalgic record (1983).*

Castle and W. Brooks: *The Book of Elstree & Boreham Wood* (1988).

Castle and J W Warbis: *Excavations on Field No. 157, Brockley Hill (Sulloniacae?) Middlesex, February-August 1968.*

Castle: *Elstree & Boreham Wood in camera* (1990)

Chauncy, Henry: *The Historical Antiquities of Hertfordshire* (1700).

Cheney, K G: *Aldenham House* (a pamphlet available from Haberdashers' Aske's School) (2002).

Chick, Avril: *The Winn Everett Story* (1999).

Clutterbuck, Robert: *The History and Antiquities of the County of Hertford* (1815).

Connell, N and Stratton, R: *Hertfordshire murders* (2003).

Cussans, J. E: *History of Hertfordshire,* Vol III (1881).

Eales, Rev. A R T: Lecture on Elstree, delivered before the members of the Elstree Women's Institute at 'Frith Knowl' on 14, June 1922, and subsequently printed.

Eales: *The First Register Book of the Parish Church of Elstree 1655-1757* (1914)

Eyles, A and Skone, K: *Cinemas of Hertfordshire* (2002)

Frewin, A and Mansbridge, J: *Elstree & Boreham Wood through two thousand years* (1974)

Gover, J E B, Mawer, A, *et al: The place-names of Hertfordshire* (1938).

Johnson, Peter: *My Elstree Childhood* (2004).

Kingston, A: *Hertfordshire during the Great Civil War and the Long Parliament (1894).*

Knee, Harold J: *The History of Radlett and its Surroundings,* a compilation in Borehamwood Library (1974).

Gutchen, Truwert, and Peters, *Down and Out in Hertfordshire, a symposium on the old and new Poor Law (1984).*

Lawrence, Andrew: *The Aldenham House Gardens (1988).* Private publication available from Haberdashers' Aske's School.

Le Neve, P and Salmon, N: *The History of Hertfordshire* (1728)

Lysons, Rev. Daniel: *The environs of London* (Vol 4, 1795-6).

Old Inhabitant of the County of Hertford: *A guide to Hertfordshire, with a history and description of the various towns and villages* (1880)

O'Neill, Bill: *The Story of Boreham Wood Football Club 1935-2005* (2005).

Perks, W H, 'My Memories of Forty Years in Elstree', *Hertfordshire Countryside,* Aug. 1971, pp 50-51

Rensten, M: *Hertfordshire brasses: a guide to the figure brasses in the churches of Hertfordshire.*

Riding, R T and Peerless, G: *Elstree aerodrome: the past in pictures* (2003).

Robertson, David: *The history of the manor of Aldenham in Hertfordshire* (1993).

Roucoux, O: *The Roman Watling Street from London to High Cross* (1984).

Salmon, N: *The history of Hertfordshire* (1728).

Sanderson, I C M: *A History of Elstree School and Three Generations of the Sanderson Family* (1978)

Smith, G: *Hertfordshire & Bedfordshire airfields in the Second World War* (1999)

Torrington, John B: *The Torrington Diaries: containing the tours through England and Wales of the Hon. John Byng between the years 1781 and 1794* (1934).

Walford, Edward, *Greater London* (1883-4), reprinted as *Village London* by Alderman Press in 1985

Victoria County History of Hertfordshire, Vol. 2

Warren, P: *Elstree: the British Hollywood* (1983).

Wratten, D: *The book of Radlett & Aldenham* (1990)

Woodcock, Benjamin. His diary while he was Master of the Barnet Union Workhouse is kept by Hertfordshire County Record Office.

INDEX

An asterisk denotes an illustration
or caption